# T E N N Y S O N

AN ILLUSTRATED LIFE

# TENNYSON

### AN ILLUSTRATED LIFE

## NORMAN PAGE

ALLISON & BUSBY

*First published in Great Britain in 1992 by*
Allison & Busby
an imprint of Virgin Publishing Ltd
338 Ladbroke Grove
London W10 5AH

Copyright © Norman Page 1992

The moral right of the author has been asserted

ISBN 0 85031 848 3

A catalogue record for this title is available from the British Library

*Typeset by Phoenix Photosetting, Chatham, Kent*
*Printed and bound in Great Britain by*
*Butler & Tanner Ltd, Frome, Somerset*

*1 PREVIOUS PAGE: Sir Hamo Thornycroft's statue of Tennyson (1909) in the Ante-chapel of Trinity College, Cambridge.*

For William Hughes

'Nobody has more fully found out at the beginning
what he was born to do – nor done it more perfectly.'

Browning on Tennyson

# CONTENTS

# LIST
# OF
# PLATES

# ACKNOWLEDGEMENTS

Thanks are due to the following for permission
to reproduce the plates in this volume:

The Master and Fellows of Trinity College, Cambridge for plates
1, 2, 14, 15, 18, 26, 27, 31, 39, and 74; the Syndics of Cambridge
University Library 45; the Governing Body of Christ Church,
Oxford 25; the National Portrait Gallery 35; the Hampstead
Museum 80; the *Illustrated London News* 62 and 77; *Punch* 76, 79
and 81; Mr Ben Page who took the following specially for this
work 6, 9, 10, 11, 17, 30, 35, 36, 37 and 82; whilst the following
plates the Tennyson Research Centre, Lincoln, appear with the
permission of Lord Tennyson and the Lincolnshire County
Recreational Services jacket, 3, 4, 5, 7, 8, 12, 13, 16, 19, 20, 21,
22, 23, 24, 28, 29, 32, 33, 34, 40, 41, 42, 43, 44, 46, 47, 48, 49, 50,
51, 52, 53, 54, 55, 56, 57, 58, 59, 60, 61, 63, 64, 65, 66, 67, 68, 69,
70, 71, 72, 73, 75 and 78

# TENNYSON FAMILY TREE

Michael T. =
(1721-96)

George T.
(1750-1835)

Elizabeth = Matthew Russell    Mary = John Bourne

George        Frederick        Charles         ALFRED          Mary            Emily
(d.1806)      (1807-98)        (1808-79)       (1809-92)       (1810-84)       (1811-89)
              Maria Guiliotti   Louisa Sellwood  Emily Sellwood  Alan Ker        Richard Jesse
                                                (1813-96)

Hallam                          Lionel
(1852-1928)                     (1854-86)
Audrey Boyle                    Eleonor Locker

Elizabeth Clayton

= Mary Turner
(1753 - 1825)

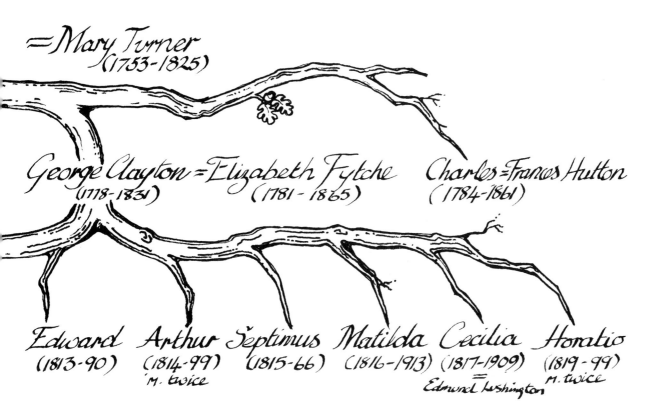

George Clayton = Elizabeth Fytche        Charles = Frances Hutton
(1778 - 1831)      (1781 - 1865)          (1784 - 1861)

Edward        Arthur        Septimus      Matilda      Cecilia      Horatio
(1813 - 90)   (1814 - 99)   (1815 - 66)   (1816 - 1913) (1817 - 1909) (1819 - 99)
              M. twice                                               M. twice
                                              Edmund Lushington

THIS SHORT LIFE OF TENNYSON, written to commemorate the centenary of his death, has drawn gratefully on recent scholarship, by which Tennyson has been well served – in particular the three volumes of his letters (which include also much material by his contemporaries), the editions of Emily Tennyson's letters and journals and of the letters of Arthur Hallam, Robert Bernard Martin's learned and humane biography, and Christopher Ricks's massive and exemplary edition of Tennyson's poems.

The illustrations have been chosen in order to present a series of images of Tennyson at various stages of his life. Regrettably, though hardly surprisingly, the material from his early years is extremely scanty, but there is no shortage of photographic and other portraits from his middle and later years, and a special point has been made of including depictions from such popular sources as illustrated magazines. It speaks volumes for Tennyson's contemporary fame that he should have been instantly and widely recognisable in cartoons and caricatures. Other illustrations show members of his family and friends, the houses in which he lived, and a selection of publications and manuscripts.

For help with the illustrations my grateful thanks are due to Mrs Susan Gates of the Tennyson Research Centre, Lincoln. I am also indebted to all those who have given permission for the use of illustrated material, to Valerie Purton and Christopher Sturman for reading a draft of the text and making numerous valuable suggestions, and to my son Ben for providing photographs of Tennyson sites in Lincolnshire.

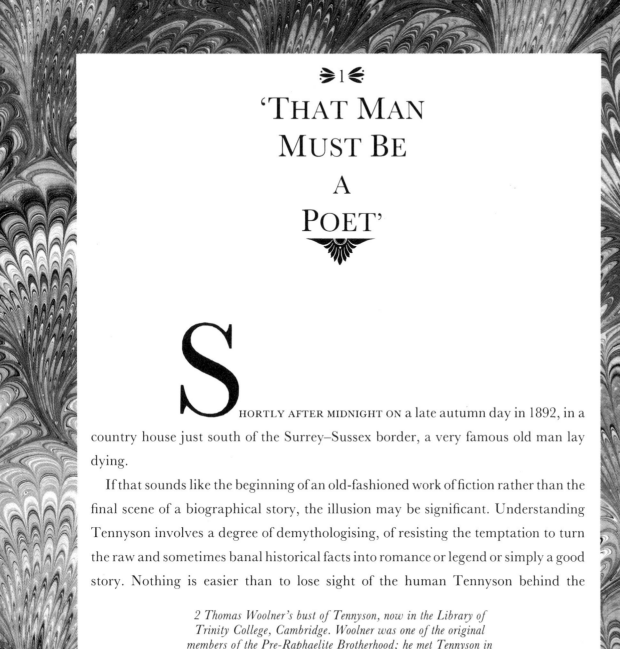

# ❧ 1 ❧
## 'THAT MAN
## MUST BE
## A
## POET'

SHORTLY AFTER MIDNIGHT ON a late autumn day in 1892, in a country house just south of the Surrey–Sussex border, a very famous old man lay dying.

If that sounds like the beginning of an old-fashioned work of fiction rather than the final scene of a biographical story, the illusion may be significant. Understanding Tennyson involves a degree of demythologising, of resisting the temptation to turn the raw and sometimes banal historical facts into romance or legend or simply a good story. Nothing is easier than to lose sight of the human Tennyson behind the

*2 Thomas Woolner's bust of Tennyson, now in the Library of Trinity College, Cambridge. Woolner was one of the original members of the Pre-Raphaelite Brotherhood; he met Tennyson in 1848 and 'was immediately fascinated by his massive head' (Martin, p. 326). Max Beerbohm's 'Woolner at Farringford, 1857' (1917), in the Tate Gallery, shows Emily Tennyson confronting the sculptor: 'MRS TENNYSON: "You know, Mr Woolner, I'm one of the most unmeddlesome of women; but – when (I'm only asking), when do you begin modelling his halo?"'*

towering figure of the Poet – an error abetted by many of those who knew him, and one that he himself helped to encourage, from his youth to his end, by acting, dressing, and speaking the part.

At Trinity College, Cambridge, there are two marble images of Tennyson. Near

*3 Somersby Rectory, from an engraving of c. 1847 (the extension built by Tennyson's father is on the right-hand side). A sonnet addressed to Tennyson by Arthur Hallam and probably written in 1830 (quoted in* Memoir, *1,66), evokes its setting:*
*Those Gothic windows are before me now,*
*    Which long have shone dim-lighted in my mind;*
*    That slope of softest green, the brook below,*
*    Old musty stalls, and tedded hay behind –*
*All have I seen . . .*

the entrance to the Chapel, for every visitor to see, and in the company of Newton, Macaulay, and others of the mighty dead, stands Hamo Thornycroft's posthumous statue, a good deal larger than life size. In an obscure corridor of the Library, next to what was formerly a gents' lavatory, is Thomas Woolner's bust of 1857, executed by a close friend. The two Tennysons, public and private, the one in a spacious and lofty hall, the other in a shadowy corridor, are both parts of the complex truth, but it is sometimes easier to find one than the other. And yet, legend apart, Tennyson's story is remarkable enough to need no exaggeration or falsification. At the same time the legend itself is, in its origins and nature, and in the range and depth of its appeal, an extraordinary phenomenon.

Let us return for a moment to that deathbed. Since Tennyson had been Poet Laureate for over forty years and in his later life had been the most celebrated living English writer, his death was to be a public event and his funeral in Westminster Abbey on a scale usually reserved for royalty and statesmen. For the time being, however, his dying was a private affair. The medical bulletin (was there ever one remotely like it?) issued after his death at 1.35 a.m. on Thursday, 6 October, depicted the last scene:

> The tendency to fatal syncope may be said to have really commenced about 10 a.m. on Wednesday, and on Thursday, 6 October, at 1.35 a.m., the great poet breathed his last. Nothing could have been more striking than the scene during the last few hours. On the bed a figure of breathing marble, flooded and bathed in the light of the full moon streaming through the oriel window; his hand clasping the Shakespeare which he had asked for but recently, and which he had kept by him to the end; the moonlight, the majestic figure as he lay there, 'drawing thicker breath', irresistibly brought to our minds his own 'Passing of Arthur'.[1]

After the body had been laid out, the copy of *Cymbeline* was placed with him, also 'a laurel wreath from Virgil's tomb'.

These details are taken from the closing pages of the official biography published in 1897 and compiled by Tennyson's son Hallam, who had devoted his adult life to serving his father. Hallam's account of the scene has strong overtones of the heroic and even the mythical: this, we feel, is how a Great Poet should die. Four years earlier, Matthew Arnold had died after running for a horse-drawn tram in Liverpool – but Arnold was not (who was?) a poet of Tennysonian stature. Tennyson was perhaps the last poet who could be referred to by his friends, without affectation or self-consciousness (and certainly without irony or facetiousness), as the Poet or the Bard. ('The Bard was very agreeable . . .' wrote Lord Houghton, who had known

*4 George Clayton Tennyson, father of Alfred Tennyson (c. 1812).*

him since undergraduate days, in a letter of 1871.[2]) The display of memorabilia in the Tennyson Research Centre in Lincoln bears labels such as 'The poet's spectacles' and 'The poet's scissors': it is a usage that might look slightly odd applied to, say, T. S. Eliot or Philip Larkin, but for Tennyson it still seems just right.

Referring to another legendary figure, Emily Brontë, Muriel Spark has written:

'All great genius attracts legend to itself. Legend is the common means of expressing the manifestation of genius in certain people, who cannot be described in ordinary terms . . . Such legend is the repository of a vital aspect of truth . . .'.[3] While this is true and important, there are obvious dangers in taking over the Tennyson legend unquestioned, and some of the details cited by Hallam may give us pause. The whole scene is almost *too* picturesque, too much like a Pre-Raphaelite painting, and the quotation from one of Tennyson's own poems (one about the death of a great king and hero) confirms the romantic and literary flavour. The full moon was an unexpected stroke of luck, but the oriel window was not quite what it seemed to be, for the house had been built in Renaissance style in 1868 (Tennyson laying the foundation stone, with a characteristically theatrical touch, on Shakespeare's birthday). As for the copy of Shakespeare and the laurel wreath (where and for how long, one wonders, had the latter been lying around?), these seem designed to contribute to the tableau. One of the problems with Tennyson's life is to find the man behind the myth, the human being – extraordinarily gifted, impressive in appearance and complex in personality, but still subject to common emotions and common weaknesses – behind the legend. Some of his biographers have gone far in this direction, and some have gone too far, for the right balance between hagiography and disparagement, between uncritical acceptance and wholesale rejection of the Tennyson myth, is difficult to attain. If enough people believe in a myth it can have the power of truth, and Tennyson enjoyed during his lifetime a celebrity that is now almost unimaginable for a writer and certainly unparalleled

That life was a long one, covering most of the nineteenth century, and his exceptionally long career embraces a wide sweep of literary history: he was born just after Byron had set out on the Grand Tour, and died when Oscar Wilde was at the height of his fame. He was an active poet throughout six-sevenths of Victoria's entire reign, and belongs with Hardy and Yeats to that small company of poets who not only go on writing to the end but produce some of their best work in old age. Yet he was also a prodigy, compared to Byron and Milton while he was still an undergraduate and tipped to become the greatest poet of the century almost before his career had begun.

For at least half his lifetime, Tennyson was a dominant figure in the English literary scene. The epithet 'Tennysonian' was already current in the 1840s. Later he was on confidential terms with the Queen, who corresponded with him and sent him a telegram on his deathbed, and he had a very wide circle of friendships among scientists, politicians, churchmen, academics and aristocrats as well as writers. At the same time he was an intensely private man with an almost obsessive dislike of publicity, sightseers and biographical intrusiveness; in his early years he showed a reluctance, by no means common among authors, to publish his work. But this combination of sociability and reclusiveness is only one of the paradoxes of his nature. His very title, Alfred Lord Tennyson, embodies the contradictory aspects, including as it does both Lord Tennyson, the public figure, and Alfred Tennyson, the private man. In his later years much effort, on the part of others as well as himself, was devoted to preserving his privacy against the onslaughts of an overwhelming fame.

The story of his life starts, however, quietly enough. Alfred Tennyson was born on 6 August 1809, the fourth of the twelve children born to the Reverend George Clayton Tennyson (1778–1831) and his wife Elizabeth (1781–1865), a clergyman's daughter, born Elizabeth Fytche, who had married on 6 August 1805. Tennyson later described his mother as possessing 'one of the most angelick natures on God's earth, always doing good as it were by a kind of intuition',[4] and certainly she needed 'angelick' patience to withstand the tribulations that marriage and motherhood were to inflict upon her. A very early poem, 'Isabel', appears to be a remarkable tribute to her qualities of mind and character.

From early 1808 they had lived in the Rectory at Somersby, a village northeast of Horncastle in Lincolnshire and one of the livings held by Tennyson's father. The Lincolnshire Wolds, not generally reckoned among the scenic glories of the British Isles, have their own quiet magic, with their rolling landscapes, vast skies, and sense

5 Elizabeth Tennyson (née Fytche), mother of Alfred Tennyson: the old painting, by an unknown artist, formerly hung at Farringford.

6 Tennyson's birthplace, the former Rectory at Somersby, as it is today.

*7 Tennyson's brother Horatio: photograph by Julia Margaret Cameron (1867).*

of the North Sea not far away. They became the region of Tennyson's early imagination, though like many who are deeply attached to a place he chose not to live there when he could live anywhere he pleased. In his later years an acquaintance recorded his unecstatic praise of his native district: 'Lincolnshire . . . was mentioned. He admired it. Nothing is finer than a plain & then a rising ground, such as one sees there, & the wild coast deserves every praise'.[5] There are enough Lincolnshire scenes and voices in his poems to qualify him as, among much else, a regional poet.

The Tennyson family is sometimes spoken of as if it were prodigiously large. The fact is that by the standards of the age it was not remarkable: Tennyson's friend Edward Lear, for instance, was the twentieth child of his parents. But Alfred and nine of his siblings were all born at Somersby, and the house (now privately owned), far from spacious, became increasingly crowded as the children grew in number and size. The first-born, George, died in infancy, but all the rest survived and indeed scored high on longevity: three lived into their nineties, three (including the poet) into their eighties, and all but one of the rest into their seventies.* Their mental health was another matter altogether. As Robert Bernard Martin puts it: 'One of Alfred Tennyson's brothers was totally insane most of his life, another suffered from some form of mental illness nearly as incapacitating, a third was an opium addict, a fourth was severely alcoholic, and of the rest of the large family each had at least one bad mental breakdown in a long life'.[6] Ann C. Colley refers to 'the family's

*The twelve Tennyson children (eight boys, four girls) were: (1) George, born 1806, died at the age of a few weeks; (2) Frederick (1807–98), who married in 1839; (3) Charles (1808–79), married Louisa Sellwood in 1836; he had adopted the surname Turner in the previous year; (4) Alfred (1809–92), married Emily Sellwood in 1850; (5) Mary (1810–84), married in 1851; (6) Emilia (1811–87), married in 1842; (7) Edward (1813–90), never married (from 1832 he was confined to a private mental asylum); (8) Arthur (1814–99), married twice (1860, 1882); (9) Septimus (1815–66), never married (the choice of his name might be thought odd, but he was the seventh son); (10) Matilda (1816–1913), never married; (11) Cecilia (1817–1909), married Edmund Lushington in 1842; (12) Horatio (1819–99), married twice (1857, 1870).

entanglement with epilepsy, melancholia, monomania, mania, hypochondria, hysteria, alcoholism, and drugs, and . . . its members' trials in public and private asylums'.[7] In a letter of January 1834 Tennyson told his uncle Charles: 'I have studied the minds of my own family – I know how delicately they are organized . . .',[8] thus bearing out W. H. Auden's assertion that 'there was little about melancholia that he didn't know'.[9]

It was a family both gifted and afflicted:

> The Somersby Tennysons . . . would now presumably be classed as, in some degree, manic depressives; they all succumbed at some time or other and for varying periods to some form of religious obsession. They all always thought themselves ill . . . None of them ever did any normal work, except Charles . . . Though only three attempted to publish, all wrote verse . . .[10]

Heredity must carry a large share of the blame for the family troubles as well as some of the credit for its talents. Socially, the Tennysons had been upwardly mobile over several generations. The poet's great-great-grandfather had been a solicitor, his great-grandfather Michael Tennyson a surgeon and apothecary who, in allying himself with the Claytons, not only married money but gave his progeny links with aristocratic forbears. Alfred's grandfather, George Tennyson, a solicitor at Market Rasen in Lincolnshire, was a successful man of business whose dealings in land added to his substantial inheritance. Having in 1784 acquired land at Tealby, three miles from Market Rasen, he extended an existing house at the turn of the century and later gave it the name Bayons Manor. Over the years he also purchased further land adjoining the property until he had an estate of some two thousand acres.

George Tennyson had two sons, and in the ordinary course of events the elder, his namesake and later the poet's father, would have inherited the house, land, and much of the money. The sons were of very different dispositions. Charles, six years younger than George, was biddable, competent and commonplace (later he was to share his father's social ambitions and to go into politics), while George was a difficult boy, alternating between moods of depression and outbursts of rage. He was physically clumsy, and well over six feet tall; though clever he did badly at Cambridge. Their father seems to have decided quite early on that his first-born would

8 Charles Tennyson (subsequently Tennyson d'Eyncourt), uncle of Alfred Tennyson: portrait by John Harrison (c. 1810).

not make a satisfactory heir: the roles of the two brothers were accordingly reversed, and the unwilling George was allotted a career in the Church – traditionally the destiny of a younger son – while Charles became the heir.

There was no question of cutting off the rightful heir with a shilling: his father intended to make him financially comfortable, and George Clayton Tennyson was

*9 The church at Somersby, restored in 1911 by the Tennyson Centenary Committee, who placed the bust of Tennyson in the nave. There is also a memorial tablet to Tennyson near the altar. The grave of Tennyson's father is immediately to the left of the tall tree; the inscription on the tombstone refers to him pointedly as 'eldest son of George Tennyson Esq of Bayons Manor'.*

never poor, though his overspending meant that financial anxiety was never far away. He was ordained priest on 19 December 1802 and two livings, Benniworth and South Willingham, promptly dropped into his lap. (These had been secured by his father more than ten years earlier, a sure sign that 'the Old Man of the Wolds' had settled the fate of his elder son while he was still a boy.) When he married in 1805 his father settled 100 acres of land on him, and in the following year he added two more livings to his collection, Somersby and Bag Enderby; he was instituted as Rector on the last day of the year. The combined income from the four benefices was about £450 – not a fortune, but with the perquisites that supplemented the stipend enough for a man recently married to live on comfortably. In 1814, now a family man on a substantial scale, he received an annual allowance from his father of £250, and in the following year he acquired the valuable living of Grimsby, worth £545. (A curate had to be paid out of this sum, but the curate would not receive much.) At about the same time his allowance was increased, probably to £500; later it went up again to £700, and by 1827 it was £1,000. This meant that from the time Alfred Tennyson was six or seven his father had an income of between twelve and fifteen hundred pounds a year, and by the time he went to Cambridge his father's income was about £2,000.

This was a good deal of money, and in those days of cheap labour the Tennysons

10 Interior of the church at Somersby. In the foreground is the font at which the Tennyson children were baptised.

could afford – or at least they employed – a housekeeper, a cook, a coachman, a valet and a governess, as well as several other indoor and outdoor servants. George's father also agreed to pay £60 a year for the education of any of his grandsons, and came to his son's rescue when he fell heavily into debt. As Martin says, for most clergymen at the beginning of the nineteenth century such an income 'would have

*11 The church at Bag Enderby, a mile from Somersby and one of the livings held by Tennyson's father.*

been riches indeed, but it seemed totally inadequate to the Doctor, who regarded himself as the legitimate heir to a wealthy man . . .'.[11] His extravagance was no doubt a conscious or unconscious protest against his being disinherited; in Alfred Tennyson's case the atmosphere of financial anxiety in his early years may have been responsible for his own chronic fretting about money, even when he became comfort-

12 Tennyson's brother
Arthur (c. 1892).

ably off, and for a streak of what has seemed to some like meanness even after he became rich.

Money troubles were not, however, the most serious of George Clayton Tennyson's problems. As the years passed the harsh fact of his disinheritance preyed on his mind and was a source of deep distress – and of far-reaching effects. As Martin suggests, 'Old Mr Tennyson's decision over the disposition of his fortune was probably the major external fact governing the first half of the life of his grandson, Alfred Tennyson, even though that decision had been taken long before his birth . . .'.[12] The younger George's outbursts of temper, abusive language, heavy drinking, frightening epileptic attacks, and later his addiction to laudanum and other drugs and his threats of physical violence, provided a disturbing background to childhood and adolescence. The situation must have been exacerbated by the fact that the house was crowded to bursting point: when Alfred was in his teens his father complained that 23 people (including servants) slept there, 'five and six in a room'.[13] The house can never have been big enough, even after an extension in the Gothic style had been built on the east side, to Dr Tennyson's own designs and partly with his own hands, in about 1819. It may be significant that some of Tennyson's most piercing early memories recall experiences out of doors and probably in solitude. Before he could read he was 'in the habit on a stormy day of spreading my arms to the wind, and crying out, "I hear a voice that's speaking in the wind"', and when he was fourteen he carved on a rock the words 'Byron is dead', having heard the news (as he later said) on 'a day when the whole world seemed to be darkened for me'.[14] Misery caused by his father's behaviour would sometimes lead him to quit the house, throw himself on a grave in the churchyard, and wish he were dead.

In happier moods, with the garden and orchard adjoining the house and meadows, brooks and woods nearby, it must have been a good place for children to grow up. Family life in that pre-railway age was very much circumscribed geographically; family holidays took them no farther than Mablethorpe or Skegness on the Lincolnshire coast. In his sunnier moods Dr Tennyson (he paid the fee for the degree of Doctor of Civil Law in 1815) told stories of his travels in Russia as a young man, stories that probably lost nothing in the telling and that must have seemed to his young audience to evoke another world than their own.

He was a man of wide intellectual interests and built up a fine library (now at the Tennyson Research Centre). Alfred, with his elder brothers Frederick and Charles, was taught Latin and Greek by his father and made good enough progress to be able to recite some of the odes of Horace from memory before he was seven. At that age he joined his brothers at Louth Grammar School, but was never happy there and stayed only four years. Hallam Tennyson writes that at this period the school was run by 'the Rev. J. Waite, a tempestuous, flogging master of the old stamp. [Tennyson]

13 Tennyson's brother Charles, who adopted the surname Turner.

remembered to his dying day sitting on the stone steps of the school on a cold winter's morning, and crying bitterly after a big lad had brutally cuffed him on the head because he was a new boy'.[15] This was the full extent of his formal education until he went to Cambridge.

Back at Somersby, the lessons with his father were resumed, but there was plenty of time for writing, and writing meant poetry. Near the end of his life Tennyson recalled that when he was about eight years old he had 'covered two sides of a slate with Thomsonian blank verse in praise of flowers . . .', and at 'About ten or eleven Pope's *Homer's Iliad* became a favourite of mine and I wrote hundreds and hundreds

*14 Drawings on the front endpaper of the Trinity manuscript of* The Devil and the Lady, *an unfinished play in the style of the Elizabethan dramatists written in 1823–4 but not published until 1930.*

of lines in the regular Popeian metre, nay even could improvise them . . .'. At 'twelve and onward' he wrote 'an epic of six thousand lines *à la* Walter Scott'.[16] At fourteen a blank-verse drama, *The Devil and the Lady*, showing the influence of the Elizabethan and Jacobean dramatists, was composed (it was published in 1930), and *The Coach of*

*Death*, a retelling of a legend in ballad style, also dates from his early teens. The picture that emerges is of a precocious child who is reading widely, absorbing a variety of influences, and imitating his current craze with great fluency and perseverance until he has got it out of his system.

He was not the only poet in the family – a happier facet of his inherited characteristics, for his father was an accomplished versifier who gave him advice on metrical composition. His brother Charles in particular shared the poetic vocation, and before Alfred was eighteen the two of them were to send to a Louth printer a proposal for a volume titled *Poems by Two Brothers*. Published anonymously on 20 April 1827 at a price of five shillings, the volume actually contains poems by three brothers, since a

*15 Receipt dated 9 February 1827 and signed by Tennyson and his brother Charles, acknowledging the payment by Jackson of Louth of £20 for the copyright of* Poems by Two Brothers.

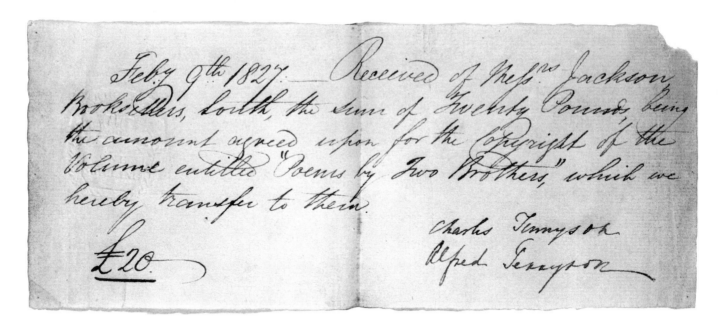

few of Frederick's are also included. The contents are predictably imitative, and Tennyson thought so little of his own contributions in later years as not to republish them in collected editions of his work. But he had savoured the delights, and the rewards, of being a published author (the boys are said to have spent the proceeds on a trip to Mablethorpe), and it is clear that, for all the severe emotional strains of the

Tennyson household, it was an environment in which creativity and intellectual curiosity could flourish. There is no reason to suppose that Tennyson would have received a better education in the truest sense if he had stayed at Louth Grammar School or gone, like Frederick, to Eton.

The emotional strains, however, were serious enough and grew worse during

*16 Pencil drawing, probably by Charles Tennyson, in his copy of Horace now in the Tennyson Research Centre, and one of 'a group of drawings which may well be of Alfred in the mid 1820s' (Christopher Sturman, 'Portraits of Alfred Tennyson in the 1820s', Tennyson Research Bulletin, November 1987, p. 16).*

Tennyson's adolescence. By 1826 his own health was suffering, and Frederick took him to Mablethorpe for a change of air and a respite from the burden of his father's presence. From this his poetry must have provided at least a temporary escape, and must in part have owed its very existence to the need to retreat into a private world. It may even have become something of an obsession. When he was seventeen he visited his rich Aunt Russell, who lived fashionably in Berkeley Square, and she wrote afterwards: 'I wish he had something in Life to interest him as well as his

17 The house in Harvey's Lane (now renamed Westgate Place), Louth, where Tennyson lived with his grandmother and aunt from 1816 to 1820 while attending Louth Grammar School. In old age Tennyson remarked, 'How I did hate that school! The only good I ever got from it was the memory of the words, "sonus desilientis aquae," and of an old wall covered with wild weeds opposite the school windows' (Memoir, 1,7). On another occasion (11 March 1890) he 'told . . . of his hating Louth School so much, that he would not go down the lane where it was, when in later life he was at Louth' (Memoir, 11, 376).

*18 Part of a fair copy in Tennyson's hand of the poem 'My Rosalind, my Rosalind', with a note apparently added later. The poem was included in the 1832 collection, where it follows 'Rosalind', of which it originally formed part. Tennyson's note indicates that he was dissatisfied with 'the rapidity of movement in the metre' of these lines and decided to omit them from the original poem; however, he seems to have thought well enough of them to publish them as a separate poem. The salvaged lines were not reprinted in Tennyson's lifetime.*

beautiful poetry – Westminster Abbey was the only thing which particularly charmed him, it suited the *pensive* habit of his Soul'.[17] The beautiful poetry was to take him, ultimately, to Westminster Abbey 65 years later.

And there is no doubt at all that he looked the part. When he arrived at Trinity College, Cambridge, in 1827 his fellow undergraduate (and later Master of the College) W. H. Thompson remarked, 'That man must be a poet.' Fanny Kemble, the actress, whose brother had been at Cambridge, recalled that 'Alfred Tennyson was our hero, the great hero of our day'. Another account depicts him in striking terms: 'Six feet high, broad-chested, strong-limbed, his face Shakespearian, with deep eyelids, his forehead ample, crowned with dark wavy hair, his head finely poised, his hand the admiration of sculptors, long fingers with square tips, soft as a child's but of great size and strength'.[18] Laurence's portrait, though not painted until a dozen or so years later, catches the image of the youthful poet. In 1827, it should be remembered, Keats, Shelley and Byron were all very recently dead, and any qualified candidate for the depleted bardic ranks would have been more than welcome. Just as Dickens was to fill the vacancy of Great Novelist created by the death of Scott, Tennyson was to become the successor to the untimely-dead Romantic poets. That he was a member of Byron's own college was a happy stroke of chance, that he later took Wordsworth's place as Poet Laureate entirely appropriate.

Alfred entered Trinity rather abruptly in November 1827 and was to form there some of the most important friendships of his life. Charles and Frederick were already at the same college, and the three brothers shared rooms in Rose Crescent for the remainder of the term, after which Alfred and Charles moved to rooms in Trumpington Street (the house still stands, converted into part of Corpus Christi College and with a window where once a doorway stood). Alfred had the promise of £100 a year from his aunt Elizabeth Russell, who had confidence in his abilities and continued to pay the allowance faithfully until after his marriage more than twenty years later.

When the next academic year began in October 1828, one of the new arrivals was

*19 Tennyson's brother Frederick: photograph by Julia Margaret Cameron (c. 1865).*

Arthur Henry Hallam, whose close friend at Eton had been a boy called William Ewart Gladstone and who was himself a son of the distinguished Whig historian Henry Hallam, whose great work on English constitutional history had appeared the previous year. At Eton, where he had also known Frederick Tennyson, Hallam had read widely and had been a prominent figure in the debating society, with strong philosophical and political as well as literary interests. Between Eton and Cambridge he had spent eight months in Italy, where he learned enough Italian to write accomplished sonnets and had developed an enthusiasm for Shelley and Keats as well as Dante. Still only seventeen when he entered Trinity, and two years younger than Tennyson, he was not only intellectually precocious but affluent, well connected, and widely travelled, so that the close friendship that eventually developed between them was in some respects a union of true minds in very different worldly circumstances. To the boy from the remote Lincolnshire rectory, Hallam must have seemed a glamorous figure. Martin perhaps exaggerates in calling their friendship 'the most celebrated . . . of the century', but for Tennyson it was unquestionably the most important and far-reaching of his long life, and Martin is on surer ground in claiming that 'It would be hard to exaggerate the impact Hallam made on Tennyson: their friendship was to be the most emotionally intense period he ever knew, four years probably equal in psychic importance to the other seventy-nine of his life'.[19]

Hallam does not seem to have met Tennyson during his early months in Cambridge – possibly he was moving in more or less exclusively Etonian circles – but after

*20 Arthur Hallam: sketch by James Spedding (c. 1832).*

their meeting in the spring of 1829 the friendship developed rapidly. By the autumn they were close friends and had already agreed to publish a volume of poems jointly. In December the two of them, with Tennyson's brother Charles, spent a few days in London together and then travelled to Somersby; it may have been at that time, or

21 Elizabeth Tennyson: the photograph was taken c. 1861, when she was about 80 years old.

perhaps during a subsequent visit the following April, that Hallam fell in love with Tennyson's eighteen-year-old sister Emily. Hallam's own family was much smaller than the Tennysons': of the eleven children born to his parents, seven had died in infancy (and Arthur and a sister were also to die young). It is not surprising that he should have been enchanted and stimulated by the swarm of gifted Tennysons. A conspicuous and welcome absentee from the household was Dr Tennyson, whose wife had temporarily separated from him the previous March. For some time his behaviour had been not merely disturbing but frightening: in a letter of 30 October 1827, Elizabeth refers to 'poor George's violence which I fear increases'; sixteen months later (27 February 1829) she tells her father-in-law of her 'most fixed and final resolution to separate from my husband as the only step that can effectually secure myself and family from the consequences of his ungovernable violence which I solemnly assure you has proceeded to such a length that I do not feel it safe either for myself or my children to remain any longer in the house with him'. Dr Tennyson's friend T. H. Rawnsley, rector of a nearby parish, who had given him shelter, describes him on 12 March 1829 as 'under the most deplorable state of mental depression and wretchedness'.[20] In May Dr Tennyson, advised to travel for his health, had left for Paris, and during the next fourteen months he wandered slowly through Switzerland and Italy, a Byronic figure retracing Byron's own travels after he had quitted England.

Family anxieties or no family anxieties, Tennyson was still writing poetry. *The Lover's Tale*, based on a story by Boccaccio and showing a Keatsian influence, was written 'in my nineteenth year' (1827–8); the first two parts were set up in type in 1832 but, despite Hallam's protestations, withdrawn from the volume of that year as being 'too full of faults' (Tennyson's phrase to his publisher Moxon), and the entire poem, including a fourth part written later and published separately in 1869, did not appear until 1879, with the earlier parts extensively revised.

In Cambridge, 1829 was a good year for Tennyson. In June he was declared winner of the Chancellor's Gold Medal for his poem 'Timbuctoo': the competitive spirit was not strong in him, but he had responded to his father's urging and submitted an entry. Hallam was among the contenders but declared himself 'delighted that Tennyson is successful'. The poem itself broke with the tradition of heroic couplets for such academic exercises – a bolder step than might at first appear

– and consists of 248 lines of blank verse. The modern reader, perhaps deterred by the title, is likely to find it difficult to appreciate the impact of 'Timbuctoo' upon his contemporaries. His Trinity reputation secured a sensational boost, and he was now thought of as a poet of enormous promise. Milnes wrote (22 October 1829), 'Tennyson's poem has made quite a sensation; it is certainly equal to most parts of Milton', while Hallam predicted in a letter to Gladstone (14 September 1829) that Tennyson

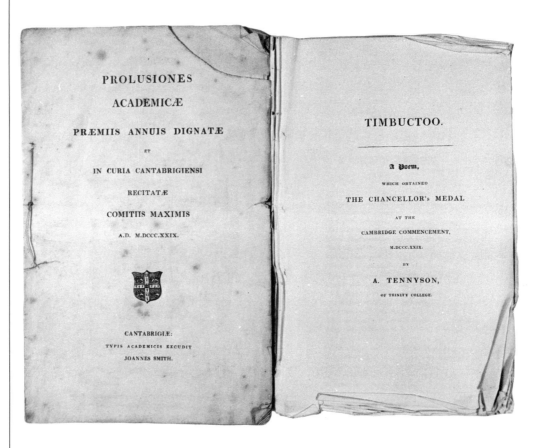

*22 (left) Title page of* Prolusiones Academicae, *a collection of prize poems published at Cambridge in 1829, including Tennyson's 'Timbuctoo' (right). The poem had appeared in the* Cambridge Chronicle and Journal *on 10 July 1829 but was not reprinted in Tennyson's lifetime.*

might well turn out to be 'the greatest poet of our generation, perhaps of our century'. These are surely extraordinary responses to a single poem, though a double-edged reaction from Charles Wordsworth (nephew of the poet) in a letter of 4 September 1829 conveys something of the startling originality of the poem as it struck his contemporaries: 'If such an exercise had been sent up at Oxford, the author would have had a better chance of being rusticated, with the view of his passing a few months at a Lunatic Asylum, than of obtaining the prize. It is certainly a wonderful production; and if it had come out with Lord Byron's name, it would have been thought as fine as anything he ever wrote'.[21] Byron had been dead for only five years, and again the question of poetic succession seems at issue.

Tennyson himself was nothing like as self-confident as he might have been in the face of such plaudits. He had had no wish to compete, agreeing to do so only after a quarrel with his father, and he felt unable to bring himself to conform to the custom of reciting the poem in the Senate House, asking a friend, Charles Merivale, to stand in for him. Later in life he was to be less reluctant to face a captive audience.

Hallam was the most important member of a fairly large circle of friendships formed by Tennyson at Cambridge. Richard Monckton Milnes (1809–85) has already been mentioned; he later became Lord Houghton, a politician and socialite, minor poet, editor of Keats, and collector of erotica. Others included William Henry Brookfield, who entered the Church and whose death in 1874 was commemorated by Tennyson in an affectionate and nostalgic sonnet; James Spedding (1808–81), who was to devote much of his life to a monumental edition of

23 W. H. Brookfield, a Trinity friend of Tennyson and Hallam who later became a clergyman and an inspector of schools: photograph by Julia Margaret Cameron.

Bacon; Joseph Williams Blakesley (1808–85), who became Dean of Lincoln; Richard Chenevix Trench (1807–86), who became Archbishop of Dublin and a well-known scholar; and two others already mentioned, William Hepworth Thompson (1810–86) and John Kemble (1807–57), the latter of whom became a historian and philologist.

William Makepeace Thackeray (1811–63) and Edward FitzGerald (1809–93) were also contemporaries but only later became friends of Tennyson's.

As this incomplete list suggests, Trinity in the period around 1830 was a remarkable nursery of talent, and most of Tennyson's circle (with the sad exception of Hallam) were to make their mark on Victorian public life. For Tennyson, the Cambridge friendships were only the first chapter of a life unusually rich in the number and range of its friendships – a fact that somehow has to be reconciled with the notion, itself not untrue, of Tennyson as moody, introspective, somewhat rebarbative in his manners, and given to fits of melancholy.

One important result of Tennyson's involvement in the social and intellectual life of the university was his membership of the exclusive discussion group that had been founded in 1820 as the Cambridge Conversazione Society but had become familiarly known, since its number was restricted to twelve, as the Apostles. At the Saturday evening meetings a paper read by one of the members was followed by discussion. The intellectual range was wide: three of the questions considered during Tennyson's time were 'Have Shelley's poems an immoral tendency?', 'Is an intelligible First Cause deducible from the phenomena of the Universe?' and 'Is there any rule of moral action beyond general expediency?' (The second of these papers was read by Hallam; Tennyson voted 'No' to the first two and 'Aye' to the third.) At one meeting Tennyson proferred the suggestion that 'the development of the human body might possibly be traced from the radiated, vermicular, molluscous and vertebrate organisms' – a startling proposition a generation before *The Origin of Species*.[22] If these gatherings seemed to be touched by priggishness and intellectual arrogance, it should also be stressed that the weekly meetings were not the whole purpose of the Society. The Apostolic emphasis on the importance of friendship was in the long run to be more important than the formal discussions. Nearly a century later, through the membership of such figures as E. M. Forster, J. M. Keynes, Lytton Strachey and Leonard Woolf, the Apostles were to have strong links with Bloomsbury.

Tennyson's participation in the formal affairs of the Society was limited, and he in fact attended only five meetings: while he had some gifts as reciter and monologuist, the cut-and-thrust of group discussion was never his forte, and he was fined five shillings for non-attendance on 7 November 1829 and resigned his membership on 13 February 1830. As Peter Allen has said, his role was a special one: he 'was never anything like a leader within the group and he was strikingly unsatisfactory as a member of the Society, but he was the only true genius they had'.[23] His formal membership had lasted only three and a half months, and his resignation seems to have been prompted by panic: according to Thompson's note in the records of the Society, 'he wrote and began to read a paper on "Ghosts", but was overcome with nervousness, and tore up what he had written, throwing it in the fire'. Thompson adds that 'He thought in poetry, and was not fond of expressing himself in prose',[24] and throughout his life Tennyson was a reluctant prose-writer for whom even writing a letter was a deeply uncongenial activity. It is hard to think of another major poet who was so exclusively and singlemindedly a poet, never writing a preface or an essay or a review, a diary, memoir or autobiography: 'He thought in poetry'.

Hallam was at Somersby during the Easter vacation of 1830 and now declared his love for Emily. Another Emily visited the Tennysons at this time: Emily Sellwood, the daughter of a Horncastle solicitor, who may have met Tennyson for the first time the previous summer. She fell in love with him during this April visit, and twenty years later was to become his wife. Poetry as well as love was much in the air that spring, for Charles Tennyson had just published (14 March) a volume of *Sonnets and Fugitive Pieces*, and Alfred was busy copying out the poems he intended to publish in the volume to be shared with Hallam. Having finished his task, Tennyson lost the manuscript and had to do his work all over again. It was not the last time he would mislay his work, and something deeper than constitutional untidiness and disorder –

*24 Part of a poem by Arthur Hallam, addressed to Emily Sellwood and copied in her hand.*

some unconscious reluctance to expose it to the world – may have been in question.

Back in Cambridge, however, with the volume printed though not yet published, the two friends had a serious disappointment when Hallam's father urged his son not to publish his poems. He may have felt that such a publication would do no good to one destined for a brilliant career in public life, and there may have been specific objections to some of the love poems written to an older woman, Anne Wintour, whom Arthur had met in Italy. The joint publication, which was to have been a symbol of the close friendship between Hallam and Tennyson, died before birth, and the outcome was the appearance in June of a slim volume issued by a London publisher, *Poems, Chiefly Lyrical*, which bore only Tennyson's name on the title page.

Tennyson was still only twenty, but it would be patronising, and short of the truth, merely to say that the volume shows great promise, for at least two of the poems, 'Mariana' and 'Song' ('A spirit haunts the year's last hours'), are among the finest of all his shorter lyrics. 'Mariana' has been described as a Pre-Raphaelite poem nearly twenty years before the Pre-Raphaelite Brotherhood was founded and a Symbolist poem fifty years before the Symbolist Movement. J. S. Mill gave it high praise in a review of 1835: 'From the very first line, the rust of age and the solitude of desertion are on the whole picture. Words surely never excited a more vivid feeling of physical and spiritual dreariness . . .'.[25] As Mill also points out with great acuteness, feeling is projected on to scenery in such a way that description

*25 Letter from Arthur Hallam to Emily Sellwood (September 1832).*

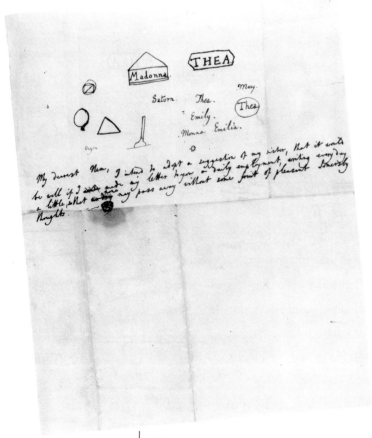

of the external world evokes the feeling. Already Tennyson has discovered, and is sounding with great sureness and power, what was to become a characteristic note:

With blackest moss the flower-plots
    Were thickly crusted, one and all:
The rusted nails fell from the knots
    That held the pear to the gable-wall.
The broken sheds looked sad and strange:
    Unlifted was the clinking latch;
    Weeded and worn the ancient thatch
Upon the lonely moated grange.
        She only said, 'My life is dreary,
            He cometh not,' she said;
        She said, 'I am aweary, aweary,
            I would that I were dead!'

Here the precision of the descriptive detail suggests an eye greedily reading the external signs of abandonment, while the sixth line refers to sound only to insist on its absence and the rhymes (including the internal rhyming of 'crusted' and 'rusted') and the repetitions ('She said', 'aweary') convey a sense of stasis and monotony, almost of claustrophobia.

The best poems in the volume indeed display a curious and disturbing consistency of mood: as Christopher Ricks says, 'Each originates in Tennyson's despondency'.[26] In the 'Song' already referred to, the refrain embodies the sinking movement from the vertical to the horizontal that Tennyson was to use again with great effectiveness in the opening lines of 'Tithonus':

Heavily hangs the broad sunflower,
  Over its grave i' the earth so chilly;
Heavily hangs the hollyhock,
  Heavily hangs the tiger-lily.

('Song')

The woods decay, the woods decay and fall,
The vapours weep their burthen to the ground,
Man comes and tills the field and lies beneath,
And after many a summer dies the swan.

('Tithonus')

The despondency was no literary pose but had mental and physical origins: Tennyson, who had already had problems with his eyesight and was severely myopic throughout his life, feared he would go blind; he also feared the family afflictions of epilepsy and madness. Later he recalled his mental sufferings during this period:

> In my youth I knew much greater unhappiness than I have known in later life. When I was about twenty I used to feel moods of misery unutterable! I remember once in London the realization coming over me, of the *whole* of its inhabitants lying horizontal a hundred years hence. The smallness and emptiness of life sometimes overwhelmed me.[27]

Shortly after the publication of his poems he was reported by his mother as being 'very ill' (he had consulted a London physician), and a year later Hallam, having received 'a very melancholy letter' from his friend, wrote that 'His mind certainly is in a distressing state'. Several favourable reviews of *Poems, Chiefly Lyrical*, including a long one by Hallam in the *Englishman's Magazine* for August 1831, may have helped to lift his spirits, but the problem was deep-rooted and the depression and hypochondria were to continue into early middle age.

At the end of July 1830 Dr Tennyson returned from his Continental wanderings, but by this time Tennyson himself had left the country. With Hallam he had set out on 2 July for the Pyrenees, travelling through France. In an adventure that anticipated the involvement of British poets and intellectuals a hundred years later in the Spanish Civil War, they and several other members of the Apostles had volunteered their services in the cause of liberty. General Torrijos, leader of the Spanish exiles in London who had fled after the restoration of Ferdinand in 1823, hoped to seize power in his native country and had the support of ardent young Englishmen as well as some of his compatriots. One group of sympathisers headed for Gibraltar, while Tennyson and Hallam's task was to carry messages and funds to a group of revolutionaries in the Pyrenees.

In political terms the expedition was a failure. For some, indeed, it was a tragedy, since several were betrayed, arrested and shot on the beach near Malaga. But for Tennyson the Spanish adventure was much more than an idealistic escapade that turned into a bloody fiasco. After they had discharged their duty, he and Hallam spent some time relaxing at Cauteretz, and 'For the rest of his life,' writes Martin, 'the echoes of the trip and his stay at Cauteretz were to reverberate through his work'.[28] During the next 44 years he returned repeatedly to Cauteretz, the 1861 visit (when he met another doomed Arthur, the poet Clough) producing his superb lyric, 'In the Valley of Cauteretz'. Tennyson never saw Greece, whose landscapes he famously described, but the mountain scenery of the Pyrenees – all the more dramatic for one brought up in Lincolnshire – became an imaginative substitute for the settings of classical myth and legend and is reflected in poems such as 'Oenone'. Sartorially, too, the trip had a permanent influence, for Tennyson wore for the rest of his life the kind of Spanish cloak and sombrero-type hat that he had seen in Spain and that had made Torrijos and his fellow exiles conspicuous figures in Euston Square. (They had been noticed there by the young Dickens, who mentioned them years later in an aside in *Bleak House*.)

The two friends returned by sea from Bordeaux via Dublin to Liverpool, whence they travelled (on 20 September 1830) by the brand-new Liverpool–Manchester railway that had opened only five days earlier and been the death of William Huskisson. By the beginning of November they were back at Trinity. The agitation that would lead to the passing of the Great Reform Bill of 1832 was already making itself felt, and some of the Apostles, including Tennyson, joined other under-graduates in December in helping the constabulary to defend the town against an attack that never materialised. They did, however, put out a fire caused by arsonists in the nearby village of Coton.

Although, according to his grandson, Tennyson throughout his life took 'a con-tinuous and vital interest in Britain's domestic and foreign politics', there are in fact relatively few explicit political allusions in his poems. Possibly his sense of Laureate decorum came to rule out expressions of personal conviction or partisan feeling. Sir Charles Tennyson plausibly argues that, though he had joined 'a set of young men with strongly Liberal views' at Cambridge, the more violent manifestations of the agitation for reform gave him 'a strong distaste for revolutionary methods'.[29] (The fact that his uncle Charles was active in the reform movement may also help to explain Alfred's mixed feelings about the Bill.) He could, however, sympathise with the aims without approving of the methods, and he helped to ring the church bells at Somersby when the Reform Bill was passed.

Early in the Christmas vacation, Hallam once again accompanied his friend to Somersby, probably to ask Dr Tennyson's permission to become engaged to Emily. For Tennyson the prospect of his best friend becoming his brother-in-law must have been a source of deep satisfaction.

After the excitements of 1830, the following year was, with a single important exception, fairly uneventful. Tennyson, still at Cambridge, continued to be seriously anxious about his health, especially his eyesight. Of external events the most momentous was the death of Dr Tennyson, his end hastened by drink and drugs, on 16 March. He died at home, reconciled with his long-suffering wife. At his funeral at Somersby on 24 March, neither his father nor his brother was present, nor had either of them visited him during his last illness, though Charles had sent his eldest son to Somersby, presumably as a mark of respect for the proprieties if not of deep concern for the dying man. George Clayton Tennyson's tormented life is deeply pitiful and at the same time appalling in what one may presume to have been its effects upon others. Had he lived long enough, he might have found a grim relish in the irony that fame, wealth and honours were to come to his own side of the family, to whose story his proud father and brother were to become footnotes. In a curious gesture, considering the torments inflicted on the family by the dead man, Alfred slept in his father's bed one night in the hope of seeing his ghost. It seems possible that he was motivated rather by a wish for proof of personal immortality (he was later to become a founder member of the Society for Psychical Research) than by a desire to see more of his father. But when all is said and done, Dr Tennyson's positive influence on his son – as father, priest, full-time teacher and fellow poet – ought not to be under-estimated. More practically, Dr Tennyson's death raised the spectre of financial problems for his dependents, for he died, as he had lived, in debt. There was also the question of when they would be turned out of the rectory by the new incumbent. At Cambridge, Tennyson and his brothers had all followed family tradition and under-graduate custom by living beyond their means and had accumulated collective debts of some £650. Their grandfather was readier to take out his chequebook than to attend his son's funeral, and he made Mrs Tennyson an allowance of £800 a year; the debts, however, were settled by means of a loan on which the widow paid interest. As for the house, the patron intended the living for his young son and in the meantime the Tennysons were allowed to rent it from the bachelor clergyman who was keeping it warm until the lad was old enough to take Holy Orders.

During this year and the next, Tennyson was poetically productive and the outcome was *Poems*, published by Edward Moxon on 5 December 1832 (but, following a common practice, with 1833 on the title page). The volume sold, or did not sell, at six shillings, for of the 450 printed only 300 had been disposed of two years later. It marked, however, the beginning of an important relationship with Moxon (1801–58), himself a minor poet for whom publishing verse was a labour of love and who was to remain Tennyson's publisher for many years. As already noted, *The Lover's Tale* was withdrawn by Tennyson at the last minute despite Hallam's protest that he must be 'point-blank mad' to do so.

One of the items in this volume, 'The Palace of Art', had earlier in the year circulated at Cambridge and had become something of a cult poem. According to Tennyson's later account, its composition was prompted by Trench's remark, 'Tennyson, we cannot live in Art,' and it dramatises a conflict in the poet – between withdrawal from and involvement in the world of action – that was to recur in various forms in the ensuing decades. Many of Tennyson's admirers at Cambridge considered that one with his great gifts ought not to be content with a self-indulgent Romantic subjectivity but should put his art to the service of the great issues and problems of the age. It was to be a long time before he seriously aspired to become 'The Poet of the People', but already the existence of the problem was recognised. The volume also includes 'The Lady of Shalott' (later much revised), 'Oenone' (begun at Cauteretz), 'Mariana in the South' (another by-product of the Pyrenean visit), and 'The Lotos-Eaters'. These are some of the most memorable short poems of the nineteenth century: Tennyson, now well beyond the stage of apprentice work, was, it should not be forgotten, still only 23 when they appeared. He is in fact one of the very few poets who not only combined longevity with staying power but did some of his best work when he was very young.

After their father's death, the question of the future arose for the Tennyson sons. There was a half-hearted attempt to persuade Alfred to enter the Church ('He said he would. I did not think he seemed much to like it,' wrote his uncle Charles on 18 May 1831[30]), but his poetic vocation was too strong to admit alternatives or even compromises: he would be a poet and nothing but a poet, and in the event he never followed, even perfunctorily, any other career. One might be tempted to suggest that a chronic lethargy had something to do with the decision, but the evidence of his creative energy is undeniable; if there was an element of selfishness in his attitude, it may have been the necessary ruthlessness of the artist.

During 1832 he continued to see a good deal of Hallam, who spent the month of March and part of August at Somersby and accompanied Tennyson on a tour of the Rhine Valley in July. Tennyson was also a visitor to the Hallam home at 67 Wimpole Street (the 'long unlovely street' later to be unforgettably evoked in Section VII of *In Memoriam*). Having left Cambridge, Hallam was reading for the Bar and still actively planning to marry Emily Tennyson.

These plans, and much else, came to an abrupt end in the following year. Hallam had had periodic bouts of illness since childhood, and in the spring of 1833 suffered severe headaches. But he had been well enough to lead a busy social life in London; when Tennyson and his sister Mary visited the city in April, he joined in some of their sightseeing and they all went together to the Zoo and to Westminster Abbey. Tennyson himself travelled a good deal during this summer: in June he was in Mablethorpe, in Cambridge and again in London, and in July he went to stay with a friend in Scotland. During this last absence Hallam paid a visit to Somersby to see Emily, making his farewells on 3 August. He then set off on a Continental tour with his father, fell ill on reaching Vienna, and died suddenly of a brain haemorrhage in his hotel room while his father was out for a stroll.

The chronology of events at this stage has a peculiar interest, humanly painful but fascinating in relation to the creative process. Hallam died on 15 September, but the news seems not to have reached the Hallam family until the 28th, closely followed by Henry Hallam, who reached England on 1 October and joined what was left of his family at their home in Clevedon, Somerset. That evening Arthur's uncle, Henry Elton, wrote to Tennyson; Matilda Tennyson, who went into Spilsby a day or two later for a dancing lesson, picked up the letter from the post office and on returning home handed it to Alfred in the dining room, where the family were having dinner. (Since mail reached Spilsby only three times a week, this may have been on 3 or 4 October.) He read it, and broke the news to Emily, who fainted away, before telling the rest of the family. On 10 October Henry Hallam wrote to Tennyson, sending his 'heart-felt and lasting affection' to Emily and asking Tennyson to meet him in London a week later. Tennyson seems to have spent some time in London and to have experienced there an extraordinary burst of creative power comparable to that which galvanised the aged Hardy in the weeks after his wife's death in 1912. His great dramatic monologue 'Ulysses' is dated 20 October.

To write a poem expressing the feelings of an Ancient Greek hero near the end of his life may seem, and is, a highly indirect way for a young Englishman to try to come to terms with the loss of his closest friend, but Tennyson said later that the poem 'gives the feeling about the need of going forward and braving the struggle of life . . .'.[31] An unconscious gloss on 'Ulysses' is provided a quarter of a century later in a letter written in December 1861: when the Prince Consort died, Tennyson remembered Hallam's death in writing a letter of sympathy to Princess Alice, the second daughter of the Queen, and told her, ' . . . when I was some three or four years older than yourself I suffered what seemed to me to shatter all my life so that I desired to die rather than to live'.[32] The alternative to 'going forward' is presented in 'The Two Voices', a poem now known to have been begun in June but taken up again and completed after the news of Hallam's

*26 Draft in Tennyson's hand of part of 'The Two Voices' (starting at line 229 of the published version), later much revised. Ricks has shown that a version of the poem had been written by June 1833, though Tennyson's reaction to Hallam's death later that year may have influenced its final version. It appeared in the 1842 collection.*

death had been received, and there cannot be much doubt that the relief of suicide was more than a passing thought for Tennyson at this time.

Also in October he wrote a number of lyrics that were to take their place in his most celebrated memorial to Hallam, *In Memoriam*. 'St Simeon Stylites', another poem combining a remote setting with the examination of contemporary problems, was written in November, and 'Tiresias' also belongs to this period, as do the lines beginning 'Hark! the dogs howl!', which Tennyson's son describes as containing 'the germ of *In Memoriam*'[33] and which includes the lines:

 I seek the voice I loved – ah where
Is that dear hand that I should press,
Those honoured brows that I would kiss?
Lo! the broad heavens cold and bare,
The stars that know not my distress,
My sighs are wasted in the air,
My tears are dropt into the abyss.

The blend of eroticism, paralysing grief and philosophical despair is very striking, and it was to take Tennyson seventeen years to develop the 'germ' into a full statement fit for public consumption. (The lines were not published in full until 1969.)

In addition, a version of the poignant lines that begin

O! that 'twere possible
After long grief and pain
To find the arms of my true love
Round me once again!

was written at this time and was to become the germ of *Maud* (1854). 'Tithonus', not published until 1860, was also begun. As these examples make clear, this short

*27 Draft of the opening section of* Morte d'Arthur, *later much revised. The poem was written in 1833–4 'under the shock of Arthur Hallam's death' (Ricks); according to the* Memoir, *it was completed by October 1834, when Tennyson told a friend 'he was busy copying out his "Morte d'Arthur"'.*

period saw the foundations being laid, largely unconsciously, for much of Tennyson's later work. Another fancy-dress poem, *Morte d'Arthur*, has an unusually direct verbal connection with the dead man as well as being the first manifestation of a preoccupation that much later produced *The Idylls of the King*. Cecil Y. Lang's assertion has a bold and attractive simplicity: 'Tennyson's whole life was a quest for a hero, and he found three . . . All three were named Arthur'.[34] (The third was Arthur Wellesley, Duke of Wellington.) Of the three, Hallam was pre-eminent in the tragedy of his early death, the loss of his exceptional gifts and high promise, and the closeness of his relationship to Tennyson. Ricks has commented that 'no event in T[ennyson]'s life was of greater importance'; Lang suggests that 'Hallam's death turned Tennyson into a great poet' (and observes, a little callously, that 'No great writer has been more fortunate in the death of others than Tennyson was').[35]

Hallam was 22 when he died. His medical history and the autopsy report suggest that a ruptured aneurysm was responsible. Before returning to England, Mr Hallam made arrangements for the body to be taken home by boat from Trieste, and while Tennyson's active pen was moving across so many pages his friend's corpse was making its slow way to England – a journey to be evoked later in *In Memoriam*. The 'Fair ship . . . from the Italian shore' reached Dover with 'my lost Arthur's loved remains' (IX) at the very end of the year, and the coffin was conveyed in a funeral cortège drawn by sixteen black horses across the whole breadth of southern England to Clevedon Court, the home of Hallam's maternal grandfather: to quote again the indefinitely quotable *In Memoriam*, 'The Danube to the Severn gave/The darkened heart that beat no more' (XIV). Arriving on 2 January, it was interred the next day in the family vault in the local church. Tennyson, who had originally expressed a wish to attend the funeral, had changed his mind and was not present.

In the Romantic tradition, by dying young Hallam achieved immortality, and the question has often been asked whether, granted a normal life span, he would have lived up to the high expectations of his contemporaries: whether, for instance, he might have had a political career as distinguished as his friend Gladstone's. Hallam's writings, including his review of *Poems, Chiefly Lyrical*, show great ability and uncommon maturity. His paper 'Theodicaea Novissima', probably read to the Apostles in October 1831, 'is generally reckoned to have had a profound bearing on Tennyson's religious thought'.[36] But if his early brilliance had come to nothing it would not have been the first or last time promise had burned itself out. At this distance in time it is impossible to assess fairly either his intellectual gifts or his personal qualities, but it is quite certain that Gladstone and others regarded him as an altogether exceptional human being. And after all the important point is that Tennyson felt to the full the Hallam magic: he was, in Tennyson's own words, 'as near perfection as mortal man can be', and his death meant of course that that perfection could never be marred.

# ❧2❧
# FROM
# CHAOS
# TO
# COSMOS

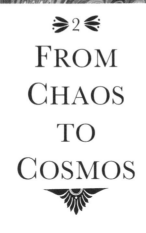

ALLAM'S DEATH WAS NOT only a personal loss for Tennyson but a bitter blow to the whole Tennyson family, which had more than its share of anxieties at this time. Emily, who had been unwell, fell ill for a prolonged period. Some of the Tennyson brothers had become unable to cope with ordinary life: in January 1834 Alfred told his uncle Charles that Septimus, still only eighteen, was 'subject to fits of the most gloomy despondency accompanied with tears'. Even earlier Mrs Tennyson had written of Edward, 'He weeps bitterly sometimes, and says his mind is so wretched he is scarcely able to endure his existence', and he had been sent in 1832 to a York asylum where he remained until his death. Charles, of whom Tennyson had written to his friend Spedding on 7 February 1833 that he 'sometimes takes some drops of laudanum by way of stimulus', was becoming increasingly prey to the drug.[37] Frederick was sent down from Trinity for eccentric

*28 Tennyson's sister Matilda.*
*She never married and outlived the rest of her family,*
*dying in 1913 at the age of 97.*

behaviour. Matilda, who had been dropped on her head as a baby, behaved strangely and seemed unlikely to find a husband (she never did). Of the other sisters, Mary was in her forties before she married, and with the loss of her fiancé it seemed possible that Emily would never marry, although she did so when in her thirties. All this amounted to a huge burden of moral and practical responsibility for Alfred.

'On the evidence of Tennyson's earlier poetry, up to 1833,' writes Brian Southam, 'it would have been inconceivable to predict the emergence of a great national poet.'[38] The crucial word is 'national': Tennyson's early poetry is self-absorbed and largely confined to a world, or rather a variety of worlds, remote from an industrialised England that was in the process of being transformed by the coming of democracy and the railways. For the early Tennyson the archetypal artist is the Lady of Shalott, weaving her tapestry in her island prison and seeing only 'Shadows of the world' in her mirror. Hallam's loss called him out of the Palace of Art and put in his hands the universal theme of grief. It was a long-term assignment, but there was a more immediate demand to do justice to what Hallam had been. Henry Hallam, anxious to commemorate his son in a volume of *Remains* (privately printed in 1834), urged Tennyson to send an account of 'the character of his mind, his favourite studies and pursuits, his habits and views . . .', for use in a prefatory memoir. Tennyson tried, but 'failed to do him justice', and, excusing himself, added: 'I hope to be able at a future period to concentrate whatever powers I may possess on the construction of some tribute to those high speculative endowments and comprehensive sympathies which I ever loved to contemplate'; it was a promise he was to fulfil only after long delays. For the moment, though he was 'somewhat ashamed at my own weakness', the subject was 'too near me'.[39]

Weakness or no weakness, there is much to admire in Tennyson at this period. At the same time that we marvel at his poetic flowering in the weeks after he heard of his friend's death we should note his impressive courage and perseverance, for the 1833 volume had been severely mauled by several reviewers – and the severity of nineteenth-century critics was of a kind to make their present-day counterparts seem timorous or mealy-mouthed. John Jump states that the reviews as a whole, though 'distinctly less favourable' than those of the 1830 volume, were 'not really hostile',[40] but most writers know that the pain inflicted by even mild disapprobation far outweighs the pleasure afforded by approval. An anonymous notice in the *New Monthly Magazine* for January 1833 (actually by Edward Bulwer, later Bulwer-Lytton) attacked Tennyson's 'affectation' and placed him with Keats and Shelley in the 'Cockney' school of poetry. This snobbish label had originated in 1817, when *Blackwood's Magazine* attacked Keats, Leigh Hunt and Hazlitt. As MP for Lincoln and an acquaintance (later a close friend) of Tennyson's uncle Charles, Bulwer must have known that the label was not even geographically accurate as applied to Tennyson, but he seems to have been prepared to use any stick to beat him. It may be significant that Charles declared in a letter that he 'had not patience to read scarcely any' of his nephew's poems, and 'never did like his affected & lame style'.[41] Much more severe than Bulwer, however, was the veteran Tory reviewer John Wilson Croker, who had famously attacked Keats in the *Quarterly Review* in 1818. In April 1833 he published in the same influential journal a long, detailed, and in many places crudely sarcastic demolition of the contents of Tennyson's volume.

Tennyson was deeply upset by this adverse criticism; it was to be almost ten years before he published another volume, and there cannot be much doubt that a reluctance to expose himself again to critical sniping was one of the very understandable causes of his so-called 'ten years' silence'. (It was not quite ten years, and not total silence, for he contributed to various annuals during this period; but the dramatic phrase recognises the strangeness of this phase of Tennyson's career.) The dislike of reviewers, later extended to biographers and literary scholars, was lifelong: again like Hardy (and no doubt many others), even when he was old, famous and rich, the frosty breath of criticism could quickly blight his life. His friend Julia Margaret Cameron described him as 'very sensitive to any critical opinion, so sensitive that I have heard him say, all the praise he had ever received didn't outweigh for the moment a spiteful and unkindly criticism, even though the criticism (he once added) was directed against the straightness of his toe-nail'.[42] Another friend, the architect and journalist James Knowles, makes the same point:

> All the mass of eulogy he took comparatively little notice of, but he never could forget an unfriendly word, even from the most obscure and insignificant and unknown quarter. He was hurt by it as a sensitive child might be hurt by the cross look of a passing stranger, or rather as a supersensitive skin is hurt by the sting of an invisible midge. . . . When remonstrated with . . . , he would grimly smile and say, '*Oh yes, I know, I'm black-blooded like all the Tennysons – I remember everything that has been said against me, and forget all the rest*'.[43]

One happier effect of the attacks by Croker and others, however, was the eventual revision and strengthening of many of his early poems, including 'The Lady of Shalott' and 'Oenone' (the revisions can be conveniently studied in Ricks's great edition).

In some of the poems prompted by Hallam's death, Tennyson speaks of his feelings for his dead friend in terms of those of a lover, a spouse, a sibling, a son – in *In Memoriam*, for instance, Hallam is 'Dear as the mother to the son,/More than my brothers are to me', while Tennyson compares his own situation to that of a widow or widower. These should probably be regarded as analogical attempts to convey the depth of his grief. In the almost exclusively male world of Cambridge it would not have been surprising if mild homosexual feelings had developed between Tennyson and his friends, but if so they seem likely to have been romantic and sentimental rather than passionate and physical: in those far-off pre-Freudian days it was probably not so much the love that dared not speak its name as a love that did not even consciously recognise its own nature. Tennyson may even have believed that his love for Hallam was, like David's for Jonathan, passing the love of women, but he seems at this period to have shown an interest in, and to have stimulated the interest of, a number of young ladies. He was still occasionally seeing Emily Sellwood and her two sisters. He was mildly attracted to Sophia Rawnsley, whom he had known

since she was a child (various members of
the Rawnsley family were to remain lifelong friends). Fanny Kemble showed an
interest in him, as did Julia Heath, the
sister of another Cambridge friend.

There was also Rosa Baring, grand-
daughter of Sir Francis Baring, a self-made
merchant who was said to be worth nearly
seven million pounds when he died in
1810. Rosa's family had moved into Har-
ington Hall, a short walk from Somersby,

*29 Rosa Baring (by
R. Buckner).*

*30 Harrington Hall, near
Somersby. This photograph
was taken shortly before its
destruction by fire in
November 1991.*

THE ROSE, on the terrace

Rose, on this Terrace fifty years ago,
    When I was in my June, you in your May,
Two words 'My rose' set all your face aglow;
    And now that I am white and you are gray,
That blush of fifty years ago, my dear,
    Blooms in the Past, but close to me to-day
As this red rose, which on our Terrace here
    Glows in the blue of fifty miles away.

The Roses on the Terrace

Rose, on this terrace fifty years ago,
    When I was in my June, you in your May,
Two words 'my rose' set all your face aglow,
    And now that I am white, & you are gray,
That blush of fifty years ago, my dear,
    Blooms in the Past, but close to me to-day
As this red rose, which on our terrace here
    Glows in the blue of fifty miles away.

*31 (a) Printed version in a trial edition, with corrections in Tennyson's hand, and (b) fair copy, in Tennyson's hand, of 'The Roses on the Terrace', published in the 1889 collection. As (a) shows, an earlier title was 'The Rose'. The date of composition is uncertain, though the death of Rosa Baring's husband in March 1889 may have been a precipitating cause. Ricks notes that Tennyson 'combines the terrace at Adworth with the terraced garden of Rosa's Harrington Hall'.*

and Tennyson probably met her in 1832 or earlier and fell in love with her in 1834. R. W. Rader has argued that Tennyson's consciousness of the disparity in worldly goods between the Barings and his own family, which formed an insuperable barrier to any idea of marriage, was the driving force behind *Maud* twenty years later. Elsewhere, Rosa's Christian name gave ample scope for rose imagery and floral wordplay, and one of the most exquisite of Tennyson's very late poems, 'The Roses on the Terrace', recreates the feelings of 'fifty years ago'. His memory, however, lasted longer than his love, for well before the time she married in 1838 he had already, as Ricks says, become 'disillusioned with her socially conventional coquetry'.[44] Not only *Maud* but 'Locksley Hall', 'Aylmer's Field', and other poems written at different periods seem to rework the basic situation in which Tennyson found himself with regard to Rosa Baring: a poor man whose genuine love counts for nothing in the eyes of her money-conscious family.

His feelings for Rosa showed that he was ready to fall in love, and even ready for marriage. 'The Gardener's Daughter', written in the summer of 1833, combines an early-Shakespearean intoxication with the freshness and beauty of the natural world (one of the girls is called Juliet) with a Keatsian eroticism. Curiously, though, its youthful passion is recollected in tranquillity, presented as an old man's memories of his dead wife. As in 'Ulysses', the young poet speaks through the lips of one whose life is mostly behind him – a way, perhaps, of keeping turbulent emotions under control. The poem's closing lines both bring forward the listener to the dramatic monologue – the reader's surrogate within the poem – and cause the depiction of young love to recede in the final emphasis on old age:

But this whole hour your eyes have been intent
On that veiled picture – veiled, for what it holds
May not be dwelt on by the common day.
This prelude has prepared thee. Raise thy soul;
Make thine heart ready with thine eyes: the time
Is come to raise the veil.

     Behold her there,
As I beheld her ere she knew my heart,
My first, last love; the idol of my youth,
The darling of my manhood, and, alas!
Now the most blessed memory of mine age.

It is also a poem rich in the one-liners, combining close natural observation with verbal lusciousness, that were to become a Tennysonian trademark: for instance,

'The mellow ouzel fluted in the elm', or 'A cedar spread his dark-green layers of shade'.

Treating poems, especially narrative poems or dramatic monologues, as autobiography has obvious dangers, but in reading the work of this period there are many moments when one is irresistibly put in mind of Tennyson's own emotional life. The slight conversation piece 'Walking to the Mail', written about 1837, contains a passage that seems to suggest that the ghost of Dr Tennyson had not yet been laid: in this poetic dialogue one man speaks of a neighbour who

> Vexed with a morbid devil in his blood
> That veiled the world with jaundice, hid his face
> From all men, and commencing with himself,
> He lost the sense that handles daily life –
> That keeps us all in order more or less –
> And sick of home went overseas for change.

Since the dead Doctor's blood was Tennyson's own, the fear of morbid devils was real enough, and his moods during these years were far from uniformly serene or optimistic. If his thoughts sometimes turned to love, marriage and poetic fame, they were also often dominated by gloomier matters. In February 1834 his brother Frederick wrote that Alfred's 'health is very indifferent, & his spirits very variable'.[45] In the summer of the same year he visited the Hallams, a dejected guest in a house of mourning. Then in the autumn he went to Somerset: at the confluence of the Wye and the Severn, not far from where Hallam's body lay, he composed *In Memoriam* XIX, already referred to; at Tintern Abbey he wrote the lyric 'Tears, idle tears', later incorporated in *The Princess*. In October he was once again at the Hallams', this time with his sister Emily. For much of the year thoughts of Hallam can never have been far away.

1835 saw a new friendship and a death. In April Tennyson went to stay with

Spedding at Mirehouse, the family estate on the shores of Bassenthwaite Lake in Cumberland. (His precarious financial state is indicated by his selling the gold medal he had won at Cambridge to defray the expenses of the visit.) A fellow guest there was Edward FitzGerald, whom Tennyson had known slightly at Cambridge

*32 Sketch of Tennyson by James Spedding, made at Mirehouse, Bassenthwaite, Cumberland, in April 1835. The inscription is initialled 'E.FG.' – i.e., Edward FitzGerald, who was also a guest at the Speddings' house. FitzGerald wrote afterwards (23 May 1835) to his Trinity friend John Allen, 'I will say no more of Tennyson than that the more I have seen of him, the more cause I have to think him great'.*

but with whom a close friendship now developed. Almost half a century later Tennyson was to make him the subject of a verse-epistle, 'To E. FitzGerald', but the humour, poise, resignation and self-awareness of the man who wrote that magnificent piece were not to be quickly attained.

FitzGerald's background was aristocratic and wealthy, his temperament passive and reclusive; the surprising thing is that a man who can not unfairly be called a dilettante, and who once described his own nature as a 'seedy dullness, which is just bearable by myself',[46] should have produced both his great translation of the

*Rubáiyat of Omar Khayyám* (arguably the second most popular long poem of the Victorian age) and a large quantity of delightful, quirkily individual letters. In later years, as Tennyson's fame grew and his style of living became grander, they drifted apart, FitzGerald withdrawing into an obscure and rather lonely bachelor existence in Suffolk. FitzGerald also came to believe, or affected to believe, that his friend's poetic powers declined after his early work. But in the years immediately after 1835 his faith in Tennyson's genius was important. Meanwhile, in the evenings at Mirehouse, Tennyson would read his latest work aloud to his friends, *Morte d'Arthur* and 'Dora' among them. It seems likely that one day the three young men called on Wordsworth at Rydal Mount.

FitzGerald's letters contain many vivid glimpses of Tennyson, and after the visit to Spedding he wrote to a friend (23 May 1835):

> I will say no more of Tennyson than that the more I have seen of him, the more cause I have to think him great. His little humours and grumpinesses were so droll, that I was always laughing . . . I must however say, further, that I felt what Charles Lamb describes, a sense of depression at times from the over-shadowing of a so much more lofty intellect than my own . . . I could not be mistaken in the universality of his mind . . .[47]

It is a striking tribute, not least to FitzGerald's own tolerance of his friend's difficult and demanding moods.

'Fitz', as he was called by his friends, was generous as well as comfortably off, and on 2 July 1835 he wrote to Tennyson from London:

> [I have] heard you sometimes say you are bored by the want of such a sum: and I vow to the Lord that I could not have a greater pleasure than transferring it to you on such occasions. I should not dare to say such a thing to a small man: but you are not a small man, assuredly: and even if you do not make use of my offer,

you will not be offended, but put it to the right account. It is very difficult to persuade people in this world that one can part with a Banknote without a pang.[48]

His tactful approach caused no offence, and it seems likely that Tennyson received assistance from him, perhaps to the tune of £300 a year, for a number of years. (Fitz was already helping Thackeray.)

On 4 July, possibly the very day that Tennyson received FitzGerald's letter, his

*33 George Tennyson, grandfather of Alfred Tennyson: portrait by Sir Thomas Lawrence, now in the Usher Gallery, Lincoln.*

grandfather George Tennyson died, leaving a considerable fortune. His funeral was a splendid affair, but none of the Somersby Tennysons turned up to witness the splendour. His will, predictably, left the bulk of his fortune to his younger son Charles; the widow and children of his elder son were provided for, though not lavishly. Frederick, as the eldest son, did rather well, but Mrs Tennyson received only an annuity. Alfred's share was a house and land at Grasby that produced a gross income of over £500. For a few years this, combined with the £100 his aunt was still giving him (not to mention the allowance from Fitz), made him reasonably well off, especially for a single man. His grandfather had, however, been a very rich man, and his will revived the old resentment caused by the disinheriting of Alfred's father; Alfred himself seems to have taken very badly the comparatively ungenerous treatment of his own family.

Old George Tennyson had lived to see the realisation of his own dynastic ambitions in tangible form. Alfred's uncle Charles, the old man's chosen heir, who had been pursuing a political career and had become MP for Lambeth in 1832, had agreed to spend half the year at Bayons Manor, and had embarked on an elaborate scheme to extend the house in order to turn it into a fit habitation for the titled landowner he expected to become. Unwilling to risk becoming confused with the *nouveaux riches*, he proceeded to create a myth of ancient origins and, by rebuilding Bayons in medieval style, a solid embodiment of that myth. The dining hall, for example, was to be 'in the old College Hall style . . . like the Hall of a Manor House of Yore'.[49] As this suggests, his plans were on a grand, not to say megalomaniac, scale, and when completed the dining hall could seat two hundred guests. Later there were, among much else, secret passages, a medieval oratory, a moat (imprudently

*34 Bayons Manor, Tealby, near Market Rasen, after the grandiose rebuilding programme conceived and executed by Charles Tennyson d'Eyncourt (now demolished). The name, with its Norman-French flavour, had been adopted c. 1811 for the earlier house on the same site, formerly Tealby Lodge; the estate on which it stood was called Beacons.*

situated on a hillside), and a drawbridge, while deer roamed the park. There were coats of arms, suits of armour (purchased from a London dealer), and a library full of recently acquired ancient volumes. To be fair to Charles, he had considerable architectural and antiquarian knowledge, and pictures of Bayons show a fairy-tale edifice breathing the last enchantments of the Middle Ages that was at the same time a genuinely creative achievement – *The Idylls of the King*, so to speak, in stone. But Bayons also represented a fantasy, a daydream, a delusion of grandeur translated into a house covering six acres: as Martin shrewdly notes, 'In both brothers there was a risky tendency to confuse fantasy and reality, and at times Charles was scarcely more rational in his dreams than poor George had been'.[50] And, pathetically – or perhaps deservedly – for all Charles's efforts, the local gentry were not impressed: one of them wrote in his diary, 'Whoever would think for all the pomp and circumstance and pretended ancestry of Bayons Manor that its owner was the son of my grandfather's attorney at Market Rasen?' He adds that it was 'the ridicule of the County' and 'an exquisite piece of tomfoolery',[51] and we may be sure that what one set down in his diary many were saying in conversation. Starting with dreams of feudal dignity, Charles had ended up as a laughing-stock.

More than twenty years in the making, Bayons Manor lasted little more than a century. It was demolished in 1964, and a series of photographs in the Tennyson Research Centre, taken at various stages of the demolition, depicts the levelling of the towers and battlements that Charles had watched rise with so much pride – and irresistibly calls to mind the fine closing lines of one of Tennyson's poems about a proud landowner, 'Aylmer's Field' (1864).

An eminent house called for an ancient family name, and Charles took steps to revive the family's virtually non-existent claim to the Norman French appellation of d'Eyncourt, from 1835 signing himself Charles Tennyson d'Eyncourt. On the monument to his father that was placed in Tealby Church, Charles refers to himself as 'directed by his [father's] will to superadd the name of d'Eyncourt, in order to commemorate his descent from the two ancient families who formerly bore that name and title'. The testamentary injunction had in fact been manoeuvred by himself, and there is something repellent about the status-mad Charles's prayer, in the same inscription, 'to walk humbly' in the steps of his ancestors. The tablet, which makes no reference to the dead man's elder son, is alluded to in Tennyson's 'Locksley Hall Sixty Years After', where old George, half a century after his death, is still bitterly remembered as 'the tyrant of my youth'. One wonders what Charles made of the famous lines in Tennyson's poem of the mid-thirties, 'Lady Clara Vere de Vere' – 'Kind hearts are more than coronets,/And simple faith than Norman blood' – if he ever read them. At least Lady Clara was 'the daughter of a hundred Earls', whereas Charles's own Norman blood was transfused only by make-believe. His longing for a title was never satisfied, but he was lucky to die before his nephew, one of the despised Somersby Tennysons, was elevated to the peerage.

There was a strengthening of the links between the Tennyson and Sellwood families in 1836, a process to be completed by Tennyson's own marriage fourteen years later. His brother Charles, now a clergyman, was well-to-do, having inherited a substantial estate on the death of his great-uncle Samuel Turner: as Alfred wrote to Spedding in March 1835, he had 'become an independent gentleman living in a big house among chalky wolds at Caistor'.[52] In accordance with his great-

*35 Memorial to Tennyson's grandfather, George Tennyson, in the church at Tealby.*

GEORGE TENNYSON ESQ<sup>RE</sup> OF BAYONS
AND OF USSELBY IN THIS COUNTY,
WHO DIED 4<sup>TH</sup> JULY 1835.
AGED 85 YEARS.

HE WAS THE SON AND HEIR OF MICHAEL TENNYSON ESQ<sup>RE</sup> BY
ELIZABETH HIS WIFE, DAUGHTER AND HEIRESS OF GEORGE CLAYTON ESQ<sup>RE</sup>
HE LEFT SURVIVING HIS TWO DAUGHTERS ELIZABETH AND MARY
AND HIS SON THE RIGHT HONOURABLE CHARLES TENNYSON M.P. FOR LAMBETH
WHOM HE DIRECTED BY HIS WILL TO SUPERADD THE NAME OF D'EYNCOURT
IN ORDER TO COMMEMORATE HIS DESCENT FROM
THE TWO ANTIENT FAMILIES WHO FORMERLY BORE THAT NAME AND TITLE

HIS POWERFUL UNDERSTANDING,
PRACTICAL WISDOM AND SYMPATHIZING DISPOSITION,
WERE A SURE RESOURCE FOR ALL WHO SOUGHT FROM HIM
AID OR COUNSEL IN DIFFICULTY OR AFFLICTION.
SELF-DENYING, BUT NOBLY LIBERAL TO OTHERS.
CONSTANT TO HIS FRIENDS, STEADFAST IN HIS PRINCIPLES,
FORGIVING, SINCERE, BENEVOLENT AND JUST,
HE COMMANDED THE RESPECT AND ATTRACTED THE AFFECTION
OF ALL AROUND HIM.
HIS REMAINS WERE ATTENDED TO THE TOMB BY ALL CLASSES
FROM THE SURROUNDING COUNTRY,
AND DEPOSITED BY THE SIDE OF HIS LAMENTED WIFE.

THEIR GRATEFUL SON PRAYS FOR THE GRACE
TO WALK HUMBLY IN THEIR STEPS,
AND PROVE HIS VENERATION FOR BOTH HIS PARENTS.
BY STRIVING TO EMULATE
THEIR VIRTUES.

37 Memorial to Tennyson's uncle, Charles Tennyson d'Eyncourt, in the church at Tealby.

36 Interior of the church at Tealby, near Market Rasen, Lincolnshire, showing the memorial tablets placed above the vault containing the remains of Tennyson's uncle Charles Tennyson d'Eyncourt (1784–1861) and his wife Frances Mary (1787–1878). (See also plate 37.) The memorials to Charles's parents are on the opposite side of the chancel (see plate 35). The church also contains numerous other memorials to members of the Tennyson d'Eyncourt family, including Charles's elder son George Hildeyard Tennyson d'Eyncourt (1809–71), who was Tennyson's exact contemporary, and his younger son, Edwin Clayton Tennyson d'Eyncourt (1813–1903), who married a daughter of the Duke of Newcastle.

IN THE VAULT BENEATH LIE THE REMAINS OF THE Rt. HONble CHARLES TENNYSON d'EYNCOURT OF BAYONS MANOR SON OF GEORGE TENNYSON ESQre OF THE SAME PLACE BY MARY DAUGHTER OF JOHN TURNER ESQre OF CAISTOR.

HE WAS A MAGISTRATE AND DEPUTY LIEUt OF THE COUNTY LINCOLN. HIGH STEWARD OF LOUTH AND WAS MADE A PRIVY COUNCILLOR IN 1832. HE SAT IN PARLIAMENT FOR 35 YEARS.

BY ROYAL LICENSE HE TOOK THE NAME OF d'EYNCOURT IN 1835 PURSUANT TO THE WILL OF HIS FATHER WHO DESIRED TO COMMEMORATE HIS DESCENT FROM THAT FAMILY AND HIS REPRESENTATION AS CO-HEIR OF THE EARLS OF SCARSDALE AND BARONS d'EYNCOURT.

HE WAS A MAN OF POWERFUL AND CULTIVATED INTELLECT AND OF GREAT POLITICAL SAGACITY: A STAUNCH ADHERENT TO OLD CONSTITUTIONAL PRINCIPLES HE YET KNEW HOW TO PROMOTE THE ADVANCE OF POPULAR LIBERTIES

THE SCHOOL IN THIS PARISH ERECTED BY HIM AND THE ADDITIONS TO BAYONS MANOR BEAR RECORD OF HIS REFINED TASTE.

COURTEOUS AND HOSPITABLE TO HIS NEIGHBOURS TO THE POOR ALWAYS CONSIDERATE AND KIND.

BORN JULY 20. 1784.     DIED JULY 21. 1861.

"Non sordidus auctor
Naturæ verique"

uncle's wishes he had changed his name to Charles Tennyson Turner. Charles had become engaged to the youngest of the Sellwood girls, Louisa, in September 1835, and the wedding took place in Horncastle on 24 May with Alfred as best man. The marriage seemed blighted at the outset by the Tennyson curse: Charles suffered so badly from nerves on his wedding day that he resorted to opium, to which he had earlier been addicted, and once again fell victim to the habit. Later the strain on his wife led to a breakdown, and they separated for many years, coming together again in 1849.

At the wedding, Louisa's elder sister Emily was, of course, a bridesmaid, and the sonnet Tennyson wrote soon after seems to make it clear that his own love and wish for marriage dated from this occasion. The poem, not published until 1872, ends:

>  For while the tender service made thee weep,
> I loved thee for the tear thou couldst not hide,
> And prest thy hand, and knew the press returned,
> And thought, 'My life is sick of single sleep:
> O happy bridesmaid, make a happy bride!'

By the following year the engagement between Alfred and Emily was a recognised thing, but their marriage was still a very long way off. It is true that Tennyson had not settled to any career other than that of poet, but he was not a poor man and could probably have afforded to marry well before 1850, so the long deferment of their union requires explanation. Since most of the correspondence between them was subsequently destroyed, it is impossible to reconstruct the early stages of their relationship in detail. What seems clear, however, is that the engagement was broken off in late 1839 or 1840. In that year Emily's father certainly put his foot down, forbidding the lovers to correspond further: to the successful solicitor Tennyson must have seemed a drifter and a poor prospect as a son-in-law, while what he knew of the Tennyson family would not have inspired confidence.

The official account in Hallam Tennyson's *Memoir* stresses external factors ('He must earn a livelihood on which to marry'[53]), but this fails to convince. Tennyson may have feared the limitations that marriage would impose on his freedom: his roaming, bohemian, self-indulgent lifestyle would necessarily be replaced by a more static, conventional and responsible existence. With a wife and children installed in the provinces, the trips to London and elsewhere would be hard to manage. Moreover, though speculation on such a subject is self-evidently hazardous, Tennyson's sexual drive does not seem to have been very powerful, and one has little sense of his being eager to marry in order to satisfy urgent physical and psychological needs. Elizabeth Barrett put her finger on the problem when she said of his poetry that 'He has not flesh and blood enough to be sensual . . . His representation of beauty . . . is rather the fantasma of beauty, than the thing. You can no more touch or clasp it, than beauty in a dream'. As Martin, quoting these words, observes, 'She had accurately sensed the deep lack of sexuality that sometimes made Tennyson's poetry seem a touch pallid'.[54]

On another level, it seems distinctly odd that Tennyson never mentioned Emily to close friends such as Spedding and Carlyle during his bachelor years: the desire to compartmentalise his life suggests that his feelings for her were put in cold storage during the 1840s. It cannot have been that the subject was too painful to mention, since the friendships predated the breaking-off of the engagement.

Furthermore, there may have been, as Martin speculates, a deep fear of transmitting the characteristics that had marred the lives of some of his closest relatives. Whatever the nature of his conscious or unconscious motives, however, Emily, who felt morally and emotionally committed to him, had a dreary wait: she was later to refer to their ten-year separation, and her lot during the 1840s was not an enviable one. She was to be 37 before she married, 39 before her first child was born. In all this some may find it hard to acquit Tennyson of selfishness and insensitivity, though his own problems during this period – including his groundless anxieties – were real enough.

As already indicated, his life at this time was to some extent footloose and

38 *Portrait of Tennyson (c. 1840) by Samuel Laurence. It was FitzGerald who persuaded Tennyson to sit, and the portrait remained in his possession until after Tennyson's visit in 1876, when Fitz decided to give it to Emily. Shortly after Tennyson's death it was repainted by Edward Burne-Jones (G. F. Watts having declined the task as early as 1884): 'the portrait today is much softer in expression than engravings made of it in the mid-nineteenth century, its prettiness far more in the style of Burne-Jones than of Laurence. The portrait, like the life of Tennyson, was changed and rearranged, in order to present a more suitable romanticized likeness of the poet to the world' (Martin). It was the frontispiece to Hallam's* Memoir *and had been first reproduced in R.H. Horne's* The New Spirit of the Age *(2nd edition, 1844). In 1863 Laurence wrote that 'delicacy and strength unite in Tennyson, more than any man I know of, and it is to be seen in his look as well as in his works' (*Letters, *II, 341), but the portrait perhaps conveys the delicacy more surely than the strength. FitzGerald, in a letter of 31 May 1881, said it was the only portrait of his friend 'that I ever cared to have', though 'it failed . . . in the mouth, which AT said was "blubber-lipt"'.*

whim-directed: he sometimes visited London, where his name had become known in literary circles, as well as staying with friends in various parts of the country. But Somersby had remained his base, and he no doubt contributed to the household expenses. Early in 1837 the rectory was required for the new incumbent, and

Tennyson was kept busy house-hunting in the London area. The family eventually settled at Beech House, High Beech, a village in Epping Forest in Essex, leaving Somersby in June, the month of Queen Victoria's accession. The new house, which still stands (rebuilt in 1850), was close enough to London for Tennyson to escape more frequently from familial responsibilities and domestic confinement. In London he saw such old and new friends as Brookfield, Milnes, Spedding, Fitz, Thackeray, Leigh Hunt and Carlyle. From time to time he and Emily met: he was probably at Horncastle in April 1838, for instance, and she visited the Tennysons in the autumn of the same year. But the distance between them was now much greater: in a letter perhaps written at the end of 1837 (surviving only as a quoted fragment) he told her, 'The journey [to Lincolnshire] is so expensive and I am so poor'.[55] It is impossible to catch the exact tone of such a brief remark: conscience-stricken or self-pitying, self-justifying or genuinely regretful. The virtual absence of the documentary record means that their meetings and their separations alike remain shadowy affairs.

Considerably more vivid are the glimpses of Tennyson given by mainly male friends. In April 1838 Fitz, who had seen Tennyson in London, described him as 'very droll, and very wayward: and much sitting up of nights till two and three in the morning with pipes in our mouths, at which good hour we would get Alfred to give us some of his magic music, which he does between growling and smoking'. Jane Brookfield, who met him in 1839, recalled him 55 years later as 'wonderfully handsome, and of tall and stately presence'. Two or three years later the Irish writer Aubrey de Vere was introduced: long afterwards he remembered 'The large dark eyes, generally dreamy but with an occasional gleam of imaginative alertness, the dusky, almost Spanish complexion, the high-built head and the massive abundance of curling hair like the finest and blackest silk . . .'. Carlyle, whom Tennyson met in 1838 or thereabouts, described him in 1840 as 'A fine large-featured, dim-eyed, bronze-colored, shaggy-headed man . . . who swims, outwardly and inwardly, with great composure in an inarticulate element of tranquil chaos and tobacco smoke; great now and then when he does emerge . . .'.[56] The Laurence portrait belongs to these years but, partly repainted by Edward Burne-Jones after Tennyson's death, depicts a serener figure than is evoked by some of these accounts, in which one has a sense of the Tennyson legend – of a figure larger than life and unconstrained by commonplace notions of behaviour – taking shape.

After his engagement to Emily had been broken off, Tennyson's life, at least so far as outward circumstances were concerned, seems to have become more nomadic and aimless than ever. He visited friends in Cambridge and elsewhere, made occasional trips to the Continent, and spent much time in London, where at one stage he took rooms in Charlotte Street, close to Fitz's lodgings. The two bachelors saw each other frequently during this period, and Fitz's letters contain some sharply focused snapshots: in 1841, for instance, he writes that

> A. Tennyson and I pass some hours together every day and night, with pipes and brandy and water – I hope he will publish ere long. He is a great fellow. But he is ruining himself by mismanagement and neglect of all kinds. He must smoke twelve hours out of the twenty-four.[57]

By the end of 1841 there were new reasons for Tennyson's anxiety. In November 1840 he had decided to invest his capital in a new furniture-making process involving wood-carving by machinery, and had paid £900 to Matthew Allen in exchange for an annual interest payment and the promise of growing rich in a short time as the new process took the world by storm. Later he increased his investment to £1,000, sold the property he had inherited from his grandfather, and added the proceeds, together with a legacy of £500 that had come to him from Arthur Hallam's aunt, to his investment. Other members of the Tennyson family – his mother, his brother Charles, and three of his sisters – also put money into the scheme.

The mastermind of this infallible recipe for wealth was Dr Matthew Allen, to whose activities there were two distinct aspects. He had been superintendent of the York Asylum in the early 1820s, had published *Cases of Insanity* and an *Essay on the*

*Classification of the Insane* (1837), and had in 1825 established an asylum at Fairmead, near the Tennysons' home in Essex, where his patients included at one time the poet John Clare. Tennyson's brother Septimus spent periods there as a voluntary inmate, and Tennyson himself stayed there more than once and was treated for 'nerves' by Allen. As madhouse-keepers went at the beginning of Victoria's reign, Allen seems to have been a man of enlightened ideas and practices.

At the same time he was an energetic entrepreneur who had twice served prison sentences for shady dealings. As a share-promoter he was obviously persuasive, though it may not have taken exceptional powers of persuasion to get the better of Tennyson's financial innocence. (Allen also tried to improve the occasion of one of Septimus's sojourns in his establishment to enlist him among the investors.) Certainly Tennyson's faith in the 'Patent Method of Carving in Solid Wood', also known by the imposing neologism 'Pyroglyph' (literally 'fire-carving'), seems to have been entire. Possibly the rash investment was prompted by the desire to raise capital on which to marry. If so, it was an appalling miscalculation that had an effect precisely opposite to what was intended. Instead of becoming rich, Tennyson lost the modest inheritance he had.

Hence it came about that 1842 was a year of impending disaster as well as long-deferred triumph, and the disaster must be laid at Allen's door. Even before the year began it was becoming clear to some that the wood-carving scheme would end in failure. On 9 May Allen wrote to Tennyson urging him to 'Have faith and all things will be more than well',[58] but faith could not move the mountain of his financial fecklessness or chicanery. By September, Tennyson, writing from Ireland, where he had gone to stay with Aubrey de Vere, was referring to 'ruin in the distance'; it drew quickly nearer, and within a few months Allen was a declared bankrupt. All that remains to be said of him is that he did the decent thing by dying at the beginning of 1845, thus enabling Tennyson to benefit from an insurance on his life.

None of this – the broken engagement, the heavy smoking, the foolish investment, and all the rest – would be of the slightest interest if the man concerned had not also been a great poet. For alongside these circumstances, which might have formed part of the fabric of anyone's life, Tennyson was leading another existence, following the bizarre occupation of being a writer, of arranging words in order and making marks on empty sheets of paper. Another of Fitz's glimpses of his friend, recorded in March 1841, shows him 'at No. 8 Charlotte Street with a little bit of dirty pipe in his mouth: and a particularly dirty vellum book of MSS on the sofa'.[59] He was, we may assume, equally inseparable from the pipe and the notebook. The outcome, breaking the ten years' silence, was the two-volume *Poems* that appeared on 14 May 1842. He had been far from eager to expose his work to the world and the reviewers: Fitz said he had had to take him 'by violence' to call on Moxon at the beginning of March, to arrange for publication, and Tennyson was despondent as he corrected proofs a couple of weeks later. (Publishers and printers worked at breathtaking speed in that low-tech age.) On 17 March Fitz wrote: 'now that his verses are in hard print, [Tennyson] thinks them detestable . . . and wishes he had never been persuaded to print'. He adds engagingly as well as accurately that 'with all his faults he will publish such a volume as has not been published since the time of Keats: and which, once published, will never be suffered to die'.[60]

Fitz deserves credit, and gratitude, for seizing the moment, but more than a year earlier Tennyson had been busy copying out his poems with a view to publication. He copied them into a book like a butcher's ledger which FitzGerald used to call his 'Butcher's Book', the edges and corners of the pages being 'often stripped off for pipelights'. (This was presumably the same as the 'particularly dirty vellum book of MSS' mentioned elsewhere; Tennyson later used a similar book for *In Memoriam*.)[61]

Moxon printed 800 copies of the two-volume set, which sold at twelve shillings; five hundred had been sold within four months of publication. An American edition, safeguarding the copyright, was issued soon after publication in London by Ticknor of Boston. A second edition in 1843 had an enlarged print run of 1,000. The collection contained both old and new poems. Some, like 'The Lady of Shalott', 'The

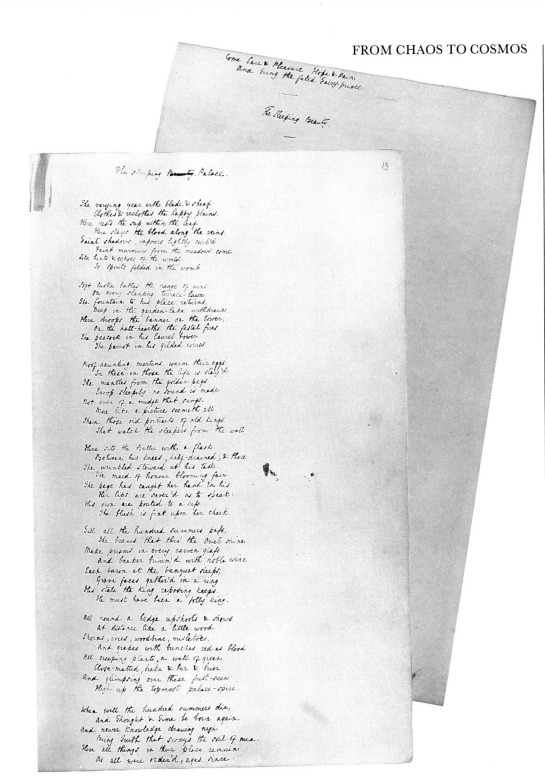

*39 Tennyson's manuscript (evidently a fair copy) of 'The Sleeping Palace', which forms part of the sequence 'The Day-Dream', published in the 1842 collection. The sequence seems to have been completed by June 1834, except for a prologue and epilogue added later.*

*40. Drawing by W. M. Thackeray to illustrate the opening lines of Tennyson's 'The Lord of Burleigh', written in 1833–4 and published in 1842. The drawing hung in Tennyson's study. Of the poem, based on a true story, FitzGerald demanded, 'Is there a greater favourite where English is spoken?'*

Palace of Art' and 'Oenone', were revised versions of poems that had appeared a decade or more earlier in the 1830 and 1832 volumes. The extent of the rewriting, and the consequent strengthening, can be seen from a comparison of the two endings of the first of these poems:

They crossed themselves, their stars they blest,
Knight, minstrel, abbot, squire and guest,
There lay a parchment on her breast,
That puzzled more than all the rest,
   The wellfed wits at Camelot.
*'The web was woven curiously*
*The charm is broken utterly,*
*Draw near and fear not – this is I,*
   *The Lady of Shalott.'*        (1832)

Who is this? and what is here?
And in the lighted palace near
Died the sound of royal cheer;
And they crossed themselves for fear,
   All the knights at Camelot:
But Lancelot mused a little space;
He said, 'She has a lovely face;
God in his mercy lend her grace,
   The Lady of Shalott.'       (1842)

Others, like 'Ulysses', 'Dora' and 'The Two Voices', had been written some time ago but never published. Yet others, like 'The Vision of Sin' and 'Godiva', had been completed relatively recently. The long silence had been a break in publication but not in creativity, which during the 1830s had been fairly continuous though inevitably more intense at some times (notably just after Hallam's death) than at others. The early 1840s were to be another matter altogether.

Posterity has endorsed Fitz's faith and his literary judgement, holding that the 1842 collection gave Tennyson a position – as 'the foremost poet of his generation' (Ricks); 'the outstanding poet of his generation' (Martin)[62] – that he was to retain until his death exactly fifty years later. Wordsworth, no less, was to anticipate these modern verdicts by hailing him handsomely as 'decidedly the first of our living poets'; Carlyle said he would read the poems 'over and over'; and Dickens was another admirer, telling Forster, who had reviewed the collection enthusiastically, that he had been 'reading Tennyson all this morning on the seashore [at Broadstairs]'; later he wrote to Tennyson 'as a man whose writings enlist my whole heart and nature in admiration of their Truth and Beauty'.[63]

Contemporary reviewers, among whom Tennyson's friends were prominent, praised the volumes but in many instances urged him to direct his gifts towards other goals. One, acknowledging that he occupied 'the foremost place' among the new generation of poets, suggested he had 'not yet become human enough'; another beseeched him to keep 'distinct and worthy objects before him, and consecrate himself to their promotion'. Milnes wrote in the *Westminster Review* that 'the function of the poet in this day of ours' was 'to teach still more than he delights, and to suggest still more than he teaches'. In another prestigious journal, the *Edinburgh Review*, Spedding said Tennyson should bend his mind to 'a great work' that embodied 'a sound view of human life and the condition of man in the world'.[64] The consensus, in short, was 'very good, but could do better'. In some of these recommendations Victorian earnestness seems already to be getting into its stride; in others, by those who knew Tennyson well, there is perhaps a hint that his productions have not yet been proportionate to his genius, and that time was passing – for Tennyson and his contemporaries were now in their thirties.

Tennyson may well have been reminded of the earlier reproach that 'we cannot live in art'. He was being pressed to renounce the withdrawn, far-far-away element in his work – the brooding melancholy of all those maidens in moated granges or high towers and those mythological figures moving in slow motion 'at the quiet limit of the world' or about to vanish over the horizon – and to write a long poem on a contemporary theme. It was, after all, the Hungry Forties, the age of Chartism and of what Carlyle called 'the Condition-of-England question'. The ideological clash was to be heard again in the nineteenth century, in the battle between aestheticism and didacticism, art for art's sake and the view of literature as a force for moral and social betterment. But by that time Tennyson himself had become identified as one of the old guard.

The development of his art in the middle decades of the century is the story of a gradual metamorphosis from lyricist to architect of large-scale poetic structures, from private mythology to public themes and contemporary issues. No one could complain that *The Princess* and *Maud* were not topical, that *In Memoriam* and 'Enoch Arden' were 'not *human* enough', or that *The Idylls of the King* did not embody a grand design on an epic scale. But before reaching a vast plateau of achievement and fame, Tennyson had first to pass through what may have been the most difficult period in his entire personal life.

The period 1840–45 was marked by a prolonged depression which, to make matters worse, was creatively barren. Practically everything in the 1842 volumes had been written by 1840; *The Princess* was not begun until 1845; between these dates he seems to have produced nothing but a few sections for the long-drawn-out work-in-progress that became *In Memoriam*. In July 1842 Tennyson told Fitz that he had not enjoyed 'a good day, a perfect white day, for years'.[65] As this suggests, and as all the earlier evidence indicates, there was nothing new about his bodily and mental ills. As early as 1832 Hallam declared himself 'very, very much grieved at the account . . . of Alfred's condition of mind and body', and added perceptively, 'I do not suppose he has any real ailment beyond that of extreme nervous irritation; but there is none more productive of incessant misery, and unfortunately none which leaves the sufferer so helpless'. Another friend, Blakesley, in a letter to Milnes (19 March 1838), noted that Tennyson 'complains of nervousness' but briskly suggested that the remedy was in his own hands: 'How should he do otherwise, seeing that he smokes the strongest and most stinking tobacco out of a small blackened clay pipe on an average nine hours every day?'[66] It does not seem to have occurred to him that what he took for a cause may have been a symptom. In February 1840 Fitz described Tennyson, who was in London with him, as 'in a very uneasy state: being really ill, in a nervous way: what with hereditary tenderness of nerve, and having spoiled what strength he had by incessant smoking etc.'[67] On 5 August 1844 Carlyle wrote to Emerson that he would be pleased to see Tennyson, who was in London again, but did not expect him to call: 'he often skips me, in these brief visits to Town; skips everybody indeed; being a man solitary and sad, as certain men are, dwelling in an element of gloom, – carrying a bit of Chaos about him, in short, which he is manufacturing into Cosmos!'

The same letter contains a fine description of Tennyson's appearance at this period:

I think he must be under forty, not much under it. [He was 35.] One of the finest-looking men in the world. A great shock of rough dusty-dark hair; bright-laughing hazel eyes; massive aquiline face, most massive yet most delicate, of sallow brown complexion, almost Indian-looking; clothes cynically loose, free-and-easy; – smokes infinite tobacco. His voice is musical metallic, – fit for loud laughter and piercing wail . . .[68]

Six months before Carlyle's letter, Tennyson himself had told Fitz that 'The perpetual panic and horror of the last two years had steeped my nerves in poison'. The medical terminology is significant, for at the end of 1843 and in the first half of 1844 he spent seven months in a hydropathy establishment near Cheltenham. (His mother had moved to that town in November 1843, living first at 6 Belle Vue Place, then, from late 1844, at 10 St James's Square.) There he had undergone treatment for nerves, and the letter continues, with the satisfaction of a patient who is aware of being an interesting case, 'I have had four crises (one larger than had been seen for two or three years . . . – indeed I believe the largest but one that has been seen). Much poison has come out of me, which no physic ever would have brought to light'. The 'water-cure', a new and fashionable therapeutic method introduced from Austria and involving the generous application of water internally and externally, was frequently resorted to by Tennyson during the next five years. It says much for his self-discipline, or perhaps for his concern at the state he was in, that he persisted with what must have been a remarkably disagreeable regimen. As he went on to tell Fitz in the letter already cited, 'Of all the uncomfortable ways of living sure an hydropathical is the worst: no reading by candlelight, no going near a fire, no tea, no coffee, perpetual wet sheet and cold bath and alternation from hot to cold; however I have much faith in it'. Probably only desperation could have driven him to undergo it, but his earlier state was truly desperate: 'I went through Hell'.[69]

The reasons for his prolonged nervous and physical collapse in the early 1840s are probably manifold. For many people the crossing of the threshold from the twenties to the thirties entails a superstitious sense of life as a suddenly serious business, of time slipping away. Tennyson was 30 in 1839, just before the onset of his gloomiest decade, and if he looked around for a moment (as he quite likely did) at his coevals he must have been aware that most had considerably more to show for three decades of living. Of his Cambridge contemporaries, Spedding, for instance, was in the Colonial Office; Milnes was an MP, a successful host at his rooms in Pall Mall and a brilliant figure in the London salons; Thackeray was a busy journalist; Blakesley, Brookfield and Trench had all entered the Church. Fitz, it is true, was a *flâneur* and a dilettante, but he was well off and had great expectations. Of his own brothers, Charles and Frederick had both married; Charles had his career in the Church as well as the Turner inheritance, while Frederick had settled down in Florence. Tennyson had no home apart from his mother's – and that was subject to frequent

*41 Tennyson's sister Cecilia, who married Edmund Lushington, a Trinity contemporary of Tennyson's and a fellow Apostle. They lived at Park House, Boxley, Kent, where Tennyson was a frequent visitor.*

moves dictated partly by her straitened circumstances (between High Beech and Cheltenham she had lived at Boxley Hall in Kent but had found it too expensive).

The debacle involving Matthew Allen had lost Tennyson his modest inheritance; only Allen's sudden death at the beginning of 1845 enabled him to recoup £2,000, thanks to the life insurance generously taken out on Tennyson's behalf by Edmund Lushington, who had married his sister Cecilia in 1842. A Civil List pension of £200 a year, granted in October 1845, also helped to make that year a financial turning point. (An attempt to obtain the Poet Laureateship for him when Southey died in 1843 had been unsuccessful.) On a more intimate level, he must have known that Emily Sellwood was eating her heart out in Horncastle; she too passed her thirtieth birthday in 1843. Perhaps most burdensome of all was his fear of inherited afflictions, including epilepsy and madness: his family's tragic history, and the present state of some of his brothers, had deeply disturbing implications for anyone inclined to introspection and melancholy. And yet, disastrous, even hopeless, as his state must have seemed to Tennyson in his frequent hours of despair, with past failures, present miseries and future terrors, it should not be forgotten that his reputation was that of 'by far the most eminent of the young poets':

the phrase is used by Henry Crabb Robinson in a letter of 31 January 1845.[70] On 10 May of that year Aubrey de Vere noted in his diary that Tennyson had read him 'part of his "University of Women," and discussed poetry, denouncing exotics, and saying that a poem should reflect the time and place'.[71] This was a notable tergiversation, with far-reaching results: the 'exotics' now disavowed included much of his own earlier work, and the next ten years were to see the appearance of three major poems reflecting, to different degrees and in quite different ways, the time and place.

One symptom of his increasing fame was the appearance, in William Howitt's *Homes and Haunts of the Most Eminent British Poets* (1847), of an engraving of Somersby Rectory. The history of poetry had become mingled with the development of tourism, and the Tennyson industry had already begun.

Yet, while Tennyson always thought of himself as a poet and nothing else, the idea of publishing his work still seemed to him a kind of indecent exposure and met with an inner resistance: in some part of his nature, writing was for him a secret activity or one shared with a few intimate friends to whom he was prepared to show or read his work. It was ironic, therefore, that in 1846 he should have found himself embroiled in literary controversy. At the end of the previous year Bulwer-Lytton had published a long satirical poem, 'The New Timon', which attacked the award of a Civil List pension to Tennyson and improved the occasion by ridiculing his early poems as effete and effeminate:

>  Let School-Miss Alfred vent her chaste delight
>  On 'darling little rooms so warm and bright!'
> Chaunt, 'I'm aweary,' in infectious strain,
>  And catch her 'blue fly singing i' the pane.'

(Earlier, the unfortunate lines beginning 'O darling room' had been mercilessly mocked by Croker in his review of the 1832 *Poems*; the other references are to 'Mariana'.) The plot thickened when Tennyson learned that Bulwer-Lytton, whom he suspected (probably correctly) of being the author of an unfavourable review of the 1832 volume, had recently been a guest of the Tennyson-d'Eyncourts, and he uncharacteristically entered the fray by publishing in *Punch* (28 February 1846) a riposte titled 'The New Timon and the Poets', in which Bulwer-Lytton's sartorial and literary dandyism was held up to scorn ('The padded man – that wears the stays – /Who killed the girls and thrilled the boys,/ With dandy pathos when you wrote . . .'). The squib, effective on its own terms, moves on to an expression of indifference to mere celebrity:

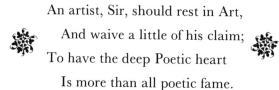

> An artist, Sir, should rest in Art,
> And waive a little of his claim;
> To have the deep Poetic heart
> Is more than all poetic fame.

A week later, still in the pages of *Punch*, Tennyson followed it with 'Literary Squabbles', regretting his involvement in the exchange and advocating a dignified aloofness ('perfect stillness when they brawl'). It was advice he was to follow with fair consistency in the years ahead, and it may be significant that many of his friends in later life were chosen from outside the literary world.

*The Princess*, published in December 1847 (and hence more than five and a half years since the *Poems* of 1842), was favourably received and soon went into a second edition; a third, with significant revisions, followed in 1850, and there were to be altogether seventeen editions over a period of thirty years. It had been begun before the end of the 1830s and, according to Fitz, was finished by 7 May 1847: in a letter of that date Fitz writes that 'Tennyson is now in London; ill and dispirited. He has finished his University of Women'.[72] Rejected titles included 'The New University' and 'The University of Women', and nothing could have been more contemporary than its theme – female education – or its setting, a meeting of that eminently nineteenth-century creation, a Mechanics' Institute, even though the locale is the grounds of a country house (based on Park House, near Maidstone, the home of the Lushingtons).

Martin's complaint that the subject is 'trivialised' is hard to rebut: it is difficult to believe that it was a topic on which Tennyson felt passionately, and a damning comment on the seriousness with which it is treated was W. S. Gilbert's ready appropriation of *The Princess* as the basis for his comic opera *Princess Ida* (1884). It is only fair to add that its sexual politics have been considered worth serious exploration by some recent critics, for at the same time *The Princess* is a poem about marriage and the relationship of the sexes. As John Killham has said, 'Whether the marriage-relationship could survive the fulfilment of women's aspirations is the real point at issue'.[73] In a passage towards the end, Tennyson puts into the mouth of the Prince sentiments that seem likely to have been his own:

> . . . seeing either sex alone
> Is half itself, and in true marriage lies
> Nor equal, nor unequal: each fulfils
> Defect in each, and always thought in thought,
> Purpose in purpose, will in will, they grow,
> The single pure and perfect animal,
> The two-cell'd heart beating, with one full stroke,
> Life.
>
> (VII, 283-90)

Embedded in this narrative and discursive poem are a number of Tennyson's finest lyrics – a sure sign that, for all the brisk contemporaneity of the new manner, there had been no wholesale renunciation of the lush, neo-Keatsian early style. These include 'Tears, idle Tears', the richly erotic 'Now sleeps the crimson petal', 'Come down, O maid, from yonder mountain height', and 'The splendour falls on castle walls', this last added in 1850 'after hearing the echoes at Killarney in 1848', and in due course making a substantial contribution to the Irish tourist industry (as a bugler said to Tennyson when he returned to Killarney, ' "then you're the gintleman that's brought so much money to the place!" '[74]).

Marriage was on Tennyson's mind at this period, and Emily Sellwood was still unmarried. On 16 July 1845 de Vere called on Tennyson, 'who seemed much out of spirits, and said he could no longer bear to be knocked about the world, and that he must marry and find love and peace or die. . . . He complained much about growing old, and said he cared nothing for fame, and that his life was all thrown away for want of a competence and retirement. Said that no one had been so much harassed by anxiety and trouble as himself'.[75] Most of these discontents are understandable, though the note of self-pity is unappealing, and de Vere was no doubt right to respond briskly: 'I told him he wanted occupation, a wife, and orthodox principles, which he took well'. The 'want of a competence' was to be remedied by the award of the Civil List pension three months later and by an income from his poems that increased markedly during the next few years. Martin expresses surprise that Tennyson should have continued to regard himself as hard up when he had, from October 1845, an estimated income of £500–700; Martin also feels disquiet that he should have gone on drawing the pension for the next 47 years even after he became rich (and he became very rich: in his later years he sometimes made more than £10,000 a year from his poetry).

In rational terms Martin's complaint cannot be gainsaid, but Tennyson's anxiety over money was only part of a complex of anxieties, and in his later years, supporting a family by the unpredictable labours of his pen, he would not have been the first or the last rich man to believe that the workhouse was an ever-present threat. His lifestyle, though dignified and even stately, was never smart or ostentatious.

In a letter written early in 1848, de Vere again noted Tennyson's crying need for emotional and domestic stability: 'He is all in favour of marriage, and indeed will not be right till he has some one to love him exclusively'.[76] That someone had of course long been waiting patiently in the wings, and in the meantime Tennyson's bodily and mental afflictions, real or imagined, continued to plague him. In the autumn of that year he was a patient of Dr James Gully of Malvern, a hydropathic expert, who seems to have dispelled his fears of inherited epilepsy, hitherto one of the likely obstacles to marriage. In late November Fitz wrote of his concern at his friend's state: 'Tennyson is emerged half-cured, or half-destroyed, from a water establishment: has gone to a new Doctor who gives him iron pills, and altogether this really great man thinks more about his bowels and nerves than about the Laureate wreath he was born to inherit'.[77] Fitz could not have realised that the Laureate wreath was after all not far away.

Then during 1849, as if preparing for the magic hour to strike, ushering in the *annus mirabilis* of 1850, events began to move more purposefully. Tennyson's unconscious, fearing public exposure of his deepest feelings, may have done its best to sabotage the impending triumph, for in February, on a visit to the Isle of Wight, he remembered that he had left the manuscript of *In Memoriam* in a cupboard in the rooms he had been occupying in Mitre Court, London. The poem, 'written in a thing like a butcher's account-book', was retrieved by Coventry Patmore, and on 2 April Tennyson read to another friend, Francis Turner Palgrave, 'poems on A. Hallam, some exquisite'. *In Memoriam*, still unnamed, was almost ready to enter the world, but there are clear signs that part of Tennyson would have been relieved if it had never done so, or not during his lifetime: in 1847 he had written to his Aunt Russell, 'With respect to the non-publication of those poems which you mention, it is partly occasioned by . . . my sense of their present imperfectness; perhaps they will not see the light till I have ceased to be'.[78]

By the end of the year Tennyson's marriage to Emily had been secretly planned; she was now living, more accessibly, at Hele Place, Farnham, Surrey. In March 1850 Moxon printed at Tennyson's request six copies of the sequence of elegies that had been in the making for the past sixteen and a half years. This trial issue was to enable him to gauge the reactions of a very select circle of friends, and one copy was given to Emily; by 1 April she had read it 'through and through and through' with 'admir-

*42 Part of the Lincoln manuscript of* In Memoriam *(the 'Butcher's Book').*

ation and delight, not unmixed with awe'.[79] It was she who proposed *In Memoriam* as the title. At last, in May, the poem appeared – anonymously, like every subsequent edition in Tennyson's lifetime, though the authorship became common knowledge almost immediately. On 15 May he obtained a marriage licence, and on 13 June the wedding took place in an atmosphere of curious secrecy: as he told John Forster a little later, he had 'told nobody, not even . . . my own mother'.[80] A poem he did not want to publish, whose (apparently) sole manuscript he did his best to lose, to which he would give no title and would not attach his name, and a marriage kept secret from even his nearest and dearest: for whatever reasons he seems to have been unwilling to share either with the world. They were married from the vicarage at Shiplake, four miles from Reading, the Oxfordshire home of Drummond Rawnsley, whose wife Kate was a cousin of Emily's; Rawnsley performed the ceremony and his three daughters were bridesmaids, but the long-delayed nuptials were an oddly hugger-mugger affair – the cake and the dresses could not be finished in time, the customary white gloves were mislaid. It was as though Tennyson were thrusting himself into the married state before he had time to change his mind.

It was at Emily's suggestion that during the honeymoon tour of the West Country they visited Arthur Hallam's grave: a symbolic act, for it was *In Memoriam* that had helped to make the marriage finally possible by reassuring her on the score of Tennyson's religious orthodoxy. And if Hallam's death had been the most important emotional event of Tennyson's life, making Emily his wife was the most important step he ever took, for it was marriage that gave his life a stability and serenity it had never known before. As he later said, 'The peace of God came into my life before the altar when I wedded her'.[81]

Emily suffered from a lifelong spinal disorder and is often depicted as slight and frail; some portraits, indeed, show an ethereal figure with almost transparent skin and features sharpened by spirituality or suffering. Ellen Terry compared her to 'a slender-stalked tea rose', Annie Fields said she had 'a medieval aspect which suited with the house [Farringford]', and Edith Nicholl Ellison evoked 'the lady on the sofa, who must never be disturbed by raised voices or noisy steps, robed always in a trailing gown of dove-colour, her auburn hair crowned with a triangular piece of old lace hanging in lappets on either side of her clear-cut, high-bred face'. There is, however, some myth-making at work here, and these pictures of a rather fey invalid

43 *Emily Tennyson: portrait in oils by G. F. Watts.* '[Tennyson] once asked Mr Watts to describe his ideal of what a true portrait-painter should be, and he embalmed the substance of Mr Watts's reply in some of the noblest lines in the "Idylls".

As when a painter, poring on a face,
Divinely, thro' all hindrance, finds the man
Behind it, and so paints him that his face,
The shape and colour of a mind and life,
Lives for his children, ever at its best.'

(*W. E. H. Lecky, quoted in Hallam's* Memoir.)

are misleading. For though she drove herself into a breakdown through overwork, she lived to a ripe old age and continued to run two large country houses until her death. Emily was no mere angel in the house but a woman of energy and determination who exerted a considerable amount of quiet influence upon her husband, even to the extent of soliciting from friends poetic subjects for his treatment. Theodore Watts-Dunton described her as a 'brilliant and stimulating' conversationalist, and she coped heroically with the stream of visitors from nearly all social ranks and walks of life, as well as (until her breakdown in 1874) with a massive correspondence. Many of the descriptions are of the elderly invalid, but for the first 24 years of her married life she played a much more active role.

A letter written by Coventry Patmore in August 1850 describes her as she was at the time of her marriage, though the description perhaps tells us as much about Patmore himself:

> Mrs Tennyson seems to be a very charming person, and I have already seen enough of her to feel that any description of her from a short acquaintance is sure to be unjust. Her manners are perfectly simple and lady-like, and she has that high cultivation which is only found among the upper classes in the country, and there very seldom. She has instruction and intellect enough to make the stock-in-trade of half-a-dozen literary ladies; but she is neither brilliant nor literary at all. Tennyson has made no hasty or ill-judged choice. She seems to understand him thoroughly, and, without the least ostentation or officiousness of affection, waits upon and attends to him as she ought to do.[82]

These reflections on wifely duty from the future author of *The Angel in the House* were addressed to his own wife. A couple of months later Aubrey de Vere predicted that her spiritual influence on her husband would be considerable:

> The Poet's wife is a very interesting woman – kindly, affectionate . . . and, above all, deeply and simply religious. Her great and constant desire is to make her husband more religious, or at least to conduce, as far as she may, to his growth in the spiritual life. In this she will doubtless succeed, for piety like hers

is infectious. . . . Indeed I already observe a great improvement in Alfred. His nature is a religious one . . .[83]

Personal fulfilment went hand in hand with poetic success for Tennyson. Nine days after his wedding, George Henry Lewes, one of the most intelligent of mid-century critics, described him in *The Leader* as the 'greatest living poet', and reprintings of *In Memoriam* quickly followed its publication. The first printing of 1,500 in May quickly sold out; 1,500 more were printed in July, 2,000 in August, and 3,000 for the Christmas trade. 'There had,' says Jump, 'been nothing like it since the period of Byron's popular success.'[84] It was to become the most celebrated poem of the Victorian age, studied, marked and digested by a vast readership from the Sovereign downwards, and to spawn a considerable progeny of exegesis and explanation – to become, it is tempting to say, a sort of modern appendix to the Bible. Its passionately argued confrontation with the implications of Victorian science (see especially Sections LIV–LVI) spoke for the disquiet of an entire thinking generation:

And he, shall he,
Man, her last work, who seemed so fair,
Such splendid purpose in his eyes,
Who rolled the psalm to wintry skies,
Who built him fanes of fruitless prayer,

Who trusted God was love indeed
And love Creation's final law –
Though Nature, red in tooth and claw
With ravine, shrieked against his creed –

Who loved, who suffered countless ills,
Who battled for the True, the Just,
Be blown about the desert dust,
Or sealed within the iron hills?

(LVI)

Its final reconciliation of 'honest doubt' with faith provided the hoped-for reassurance:

No longer half-akin to brute,
    For all we thought and loved and did,
    And hoped, and suffered, is but seed
Of what in them is flower and fruit;

Whereof the man, that with me trod
    This planet, was a noble type
    Appearing ere the times were ripe,
That friend of mine who lives in God,

That God, which ever lives and loves,
    One God, one law, one element,
    And one far-off divine event,
To which the whole creation moves.

(Epilogue)

*In Memoriam* is at the same time an intensely personal poem, deriving its impulse and power from the most important emotional crisis of Tennyson's life, and a public poem that found an echo in nearly every middle-class bosom.

That year, 1850, had all the qualifications to be a magical year and a boost to the wavering faith of numerologists. The midpoint of the century, almost precisely the midpoint of Tennyson's own life, it saw the pivotal event of his marriage and the poem that brought him great fame. And its wonders were not yet exhausted: Wordsworth had died on 23 April, during the summer *Punch* was deploring official tardiness in announcing his successor,[85] and on 5 November Tennyson was offered the Laureateship. The arrival of the letter from the Keeper of Her Majesty's Privy Purse on 9 November came hard on the heels of a dream that lends itself almost too eagerly to Freudian interpretation: the previous night, it seems, Tennyson had dreamed 'that the Queen and the Prince had called on him at his Mother's and been very gracious, the Prince kissing him, which made him think "very kind but very German"'.[86] If his mother's house represented the pre-nuptial past, Albert may have stood in for another A, Arthur Hallam, who had died in a German-speaking country and whose death had indirectly been the source of his present success. He accepted the Laureateship on 13 November with the stipulation that 'no birthday ode should be required' – the fear of being forced into publication was still potent – and the official announcement was made on the 19th. He was to hold the office for almost 42 years, through two-thirds of Victoria's entire reign.

It is no exaggeration to say that Tennyson's life was transformed by the events of 1850. There was initially an unsettled period of honeymooning and house-hunting, but soon his lifestyle acquired an order and stability that it had never possessed before. Emily Tennyson is one of those literary wives (Carrie Kipling is another) who saw her role as being the creation of the conditions in which her husband's genius could fulfil itself. She may, as some have urged, have tamed Tennyson, turning the romantic rebel into a bourgeois paterfamilias and a pillar of the establishment; she certainly rescued him from depression and hypochondria and helped him to outwit Dr Gully's prognosis that he 'wd. probably have some Paralysis at about 55: but, if he went on smoking, *sooner*'.[87] His attendance at a levee or Court reception on 6 March 1851 was in its small way emblematic of the change: the erstwhile moody wanderer had accepted a recognised place in society, like Wordsworth becoming Stamp Distributor for Westmorland. For the occasion he frugally borrowed Samuel Rogers's court dress, which had also been worn by Wordsworth; the jacket fitted tolerably well, but the trousers caused 'some anxiety'.[88]

Just how much Tennyson was changed by marriage, or how much it stirred dormant aspects of his nature, is shown by his reaction to fatherhood. His first child was still-born on 20 April 1851, which by a painful irony was Easter Sunday. Several of the many letters he wrote at the time have survived, and in them his prose has an emotional power it does not often possess or aspire to: 'He was – not born, I cannot call it born for he never breathed – but he was released from the prison where he moved for nine months – on Easter Sunday'; 'The whole night before he was born he was vigorously alive, but in being born he died'; 'The nurse drest up the little body in pure white. He was a grand, massive, manchild, noble brow, and hands, which he had clenched as in his determination to be born. Had he lived the doctor said he would have been lusty and healthy, but somehow he got strangled'.[89] Three years later, when he had a son of nearly two 'toddling up and down the room', the pain was still vivid: 'I nearly broke my heart with going to look at him. He lay like a little warrior, having fought the fight and failed, with his hands clenched, and a frown on his brow . . . If my latest-born were to die to-night, I do not think that I should suffer so much as I did, looking on that noble fellow who had never seen the light'.[90] It is not, perhaps, a reaction for which anything in Tennyson's earlier life prepares us.

The toddler in the spring of 1854 was the inevitably named Hallam, born prematurely on 11 August 1852; Henry Hallam became his godfather. Hallam was to become his father's secretary and biographer, to have a distinguished public career (culminating in the Governor-Generalship of Australia) after his father's death, and to live until 1928. On the day of his birth Tennyson wrote to Forster: 'I have seen beautiful things in my life, but I never saw anything more beautiful than the mother's face as she lay by the young child an hour or two after, or heard anything sweeter than the little lamblike bleat of the young one'. A few days later he told de Vere: 'I was rather awestruck by him on his third day of life. I went into the nursery to look at him as he was lying alone and while I was regarding him I found that he was earnestly regarding me with wide open eyes in perfect silence. I felt as if I had seen a spirit . . .' But in the same letter, cheek by jowl with this fascinated response to a moving and wholly new experience, is an engaging whimsicality: 'Such a roar he sets up if he cannot get the milk in a moment out of the breast, such a lamentation if his little demi-bald sconce has to be brushed with a brush that would not bruise a midge'.[91] Tennyson's letters do not often show such vivacity, such

*44 Chapel House, Twickenham, where the Tennysons lived in 1851–2.*

concern to catch the precious flavour of the moment: the new though far from young father (he had just passed his 43rd birthday) has been touched to the depths by this tiny peremptory invader of his life. Fitz provides a glimpse of him at the end of the year, 'nurs[ing the baby] with humour and majesty'.[92]

From the spring of 1851 they had been living at Chapel House, Twickenham, but its associations with the dead child had made it uncongenial and by the spring of

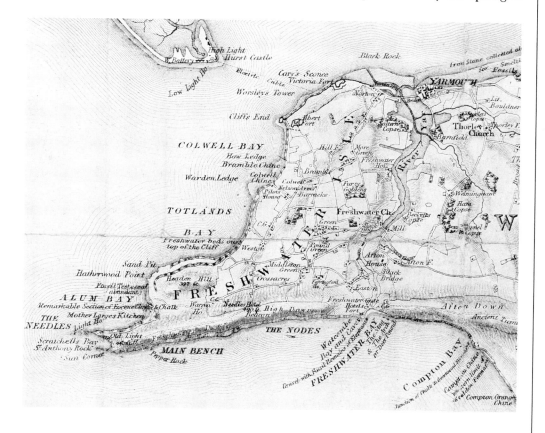

*45 Part of* Stanford's Tourist's Map of the Isle of Wight *(1860). Farringford, separated from the sea-coast by High Down, is northwest of Freshwater Bay.*

1852 they were house-hunting again, this time looking for a country residence. It was not, however, until the autumn of the next year that Tennyson discovered Farringford on the Isle of Wight. Its isolation and the magnificence of the nearby views appealed to him, though the financial commitment aroused old anxieties ('I rather shake under the fear of being ruined'[93]). In November he signed a lease for three years with the option to purchase when the lease expired. His worries seemed misplaced in relation to the modest rent – two pounds a week for a furnished country house – and his increasing prosperity (Moxon paid him a thousand pounds before they even moved in); but then Tennyson was no stranger to irrational anxieties. At

46 Drawing of Farringford by Edward Lear, dated 15 October 1864. Lear wrote in his diary during this visit, 'Altogether this is one of the places I am really happy in (and few they are) – though the pleasure is mingled with melancholy . . . Emily T. is I think sadder than formerly . . . Alfred is more expansive and offensive than usual.'

the time of the move Emily was pregnant again, and their second son, Lionel, was born at Farringford on 16 March 1854. As so often in Tennyson's life, chance supplied poetically or dramatically felicitous circumstances: when he heard that the child was born, Tennyson was watching the stars (a favourite pastime) and, in Emily's phrase, 'saw Mars in the Lion culminating' – hence the boy's name.[94]

He had accepted the Laureateship with the careful proviso that ceremonial or court poems written to order were not to be demanded from him, but wider events were soon to inspire two of his best-known public poems and to further the transformation of the solitary dreamer into a public figure. The Duke of Wellington had been the national hero of Tennyson's early childhood. His death on 14 September 1852 produced an explosion of patriotic and nostalgic sentiment: as Dickens wrote on 23 September, the public seemed 'to have gone mad about the funeral'.[95] The crowd watching the procession that wended its way to St Paul's on 18 November was estimated at one and a half million, and Tennyson was among them. His 'Ode on the Death of the Duke of Wellington' had been published two days earlier after being composed in fair haste, and some of the 10,000 copies printed were sold to the crowd. Tennyson, who had received £200 from Moxon for the poem, took the opportunity of a second edition early in 1853 to add 29 lines and to make numerous revisions.

Two years later, the notorious Charge of the Light Brigade in the Crimea (25 October 1854) was responsible for a poem of which everyone has heard even if they have never opened a volume of Tennyson – though he himself was soon to dismiss it as 'Not a poem on which I pique myself'.[96] The *Times* editorial of 13 November had used the phrase 'some hideous blunder', transmuted in the poem into the now-proverbial 'Some one had blundered'. The repeated reference to 'the six hundred' is a poetic approximation that caused Tennyson some trouble: according to Emily's letter to Forster, in whose weekly *Examiner* the poem appeared on 9 December, Tennyson preferred 'six hundred' 'on account of the metre', even though *The Times* had referred to 'about 700' (a further report the next day gave the amended figure of 607, but a modern historian's calculation is 673).

Both poems are in an orotund style – *allegro moderato* in the 'Charge', *andante maestoso* in the 'Ode' – that is very different from the characteristic voices of Tennyson's earlier poems:

> 'Forward, the Light Brigade!'
> Was there a man dismayed?
> Not though the soldier knew

Some one had blundered;
Their's not to make reply,
Their's not to reason why,
Their's but to do and die:
Into the valley of Death
Rode the six hundred.

Lead out the pageant: sad and slow,
As fits an universal woe,
Let the long long procession go,
And let the sorrowing crowd about it grow,
And let the mournful martial music blow;
The last great Englishman is low.

*Maud*, published on 28 July 1855, is a more radical experiment and was judged a failure by many contemporaries. It is in fact one of those classics, so readily accessible to the modern reader, that disconcerted or disgusted its own age in a way that cannot be understood without a considerable effort of the historical imagination. Gladstone, who found the 'Ode' 'worthy of . . . its immortal subject', judged *Maud* 'unintelligible', though like others he was later to change his mind.[97] Sir Charles Tennyson has described the 'almost universal reprobation' with which it was received:

'Obscurity taken for profundity,' 'the dead level of prose run mad,' 'rampant and rabid bloodthirstiness of soul,' were a few of the descriptions lavished on it by the reviewers. One critic commented that one of the two vowels should be omitted from the title, and that it didn't much matter which was chosen for the purpose. Another said, 'If an author pipe of adultery, fornication, murder and suicide, set him down as the practiser of those crimes.' This time Alfred's sense

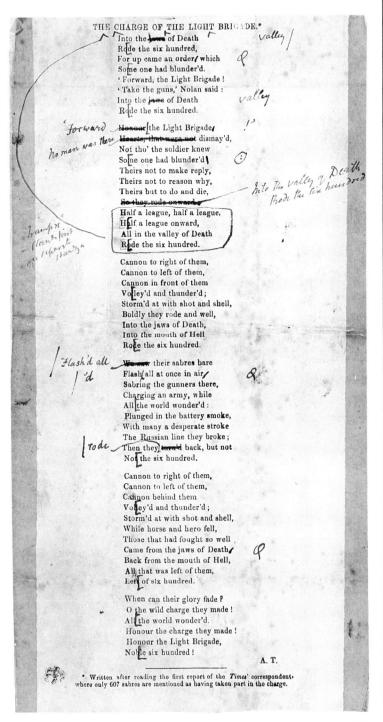

47 *Galley proof of 'The Charge of the Light Brigade', published in* The Examiner *on 9 December 1854 (signed 'A.T.') after being written 'in a few minutes' on 2 December. Tennyson had read the reports in* The Times *(see his footnote) published on 13 and 14 November. The rhyming of 'thunder'd' and 'hundred' suggests that Tennyson may have pronounced the latter word in the Lincolnshire manner ('hunderd').*

of humour was equal to the occasion and he replied: 'Adulterer I may be, fornicator I may be, murderer I may be, suicide I am not yet.'[98]

The origins of *Maud*, like those of *In Memoriam*, went back a long way. As already noted, one of the poetic reactions to Hallam's death had been a fragment later expanded and published in 1837 as 'Stanzas', beginning 'Oh! that 'twere possible,/ After long grief and pain,/ To find the arms of my true love/ Round me once again!' R. W. Rader's study of the poem's biographical sources argues that *Maud* embodies many of the main elements of Tennyson's early life, including the difficult father, the *arriviste* relative who had built a 'gewgaw castle', the fear of madness, and the unhappy love affair with Rosa Baring: 'the loss of Hallam generated the need for the substitutive love which, in the quick succession of four years, Tennyson sought in Rosa, and then in Sophy [Rawnsley] and Emily [Sellwood]'.[99] Tennyson himself, as reported by his son, declared that 'This poem of *Maud or the Madness* is a little *Hamlet*, the history of a morbid, poetic soul, under the blighting influence of a recklessly speculative age'.[100]

He added: 'The peculiarity of this poem is that different phases of passion in one person take the place of different characters', and this explains the subtitle 'A Monodrama'. The tense, nervous rhythms of the opening lines set the tone:

> I hate the dreadful hollow behind the little wood,
> Its lips in the field above are dabbled with blood-red heath,
> The red-ribbed ledges drip with a silent horror of blood,
> And Echo there, whatever is asked her, answers 'Death.'

This is very different from the measured, meditative flow and ebb of the *In Memoriam* stanza, and there are lines in the poem that have a very modern kind of intensity that derives from a rich ambiguity: 'And the flying gold of the ruined woodlands drove through the air'. At times we seem to be in the world of T. S. Eliot's early verse:

Then I rise, the eavedrops fall,
And the yellow vapours choke
The great city sounding wide;
The day comes, a dull red ball
Wrapt in drifts of lurid smoke
On the misty river-tide.

And again:

And I loathe the squares and streets,
And the faces that one meets . . .
And my heart is a handful of dust

– that last phrase duly turning up, of course, in *The Waste Land* as well as providing the title of one of Evelyn Waugh's novels.

*Maud* offers not only the exploration of a morbid subjectivity, breakdown, and healing, but touches on a remarkably diverse list of contemporary issues, including wife-beating, poor housing conditions, the adulteration of food, child-murder, and, in one splendid passage, the breathtaking implications of the new geology:

A monstrous eft was of old the Lord and Master of Earth,
For him did his high sun flame, and his river billowing ran,
And he felt himself in his force to be Nature's crowning race.
As nine months go to the shaping an infant ripe for his birth,
So many a million of ages have gone to the making of man:
He now is first, but is he the last? is he not too base?

(IV, vi)

At the same time it is a poem of dizzying metrical variety and virtuosity with some highly effective shifts of mood and tone: at times close to rant, it can also be exquisitely lyrical, as in 'See what a lovely shell' at the beginning of Part II, and (if we can manage to forget the generations of stout baritones who have 'rendered' it) 'Come into the garden, Maud' a little earlier.

Many of the first readers of *Maud*, confusing speaker with poet, found the bellicose and jingoistic ending particularly repugnant:

> For the peace, that I deemed no peace, is over and done,
> And now by the side of the Black and the Baltic deep,
> And deathful-grinning mouths of the fortress, flames
> The blood-red blossom of war with a heart of fire.
>
> Let it flame or fade, and the war roll down like a wind,
> We have proved we have hearts in a cause, we are noble still,
> And myself have awaked, as it seems, to the better mind;
> It is better to fight for the good than to rail at the ill;
> I have felt with my native land, I am one with my kind,
> I embrace the purpose of God, and the doom assigned.

In the *Westminster Review*, George Eliot remarked acidly that she could not share Tennyson's faith in 'War as the unique social regenerator', while Goldwin Smith in the *Saturday Review* likewise condemned the poem's 'glorification of war'.[101] Disapproval or no disapproval, *Maud* became a favourite child of Tennyson's (to use the phrase that Dickens used of his own feelings for *David Copperfield*, another autobiographical fiction), and, perhaps because its personal associations were combined with rhetorical effectiveness, it became the poem he especially liked to read aloud or recite. Even that much-abused word 'obsession' is hardly too strong for his proclivity to get visitors into a corner and give them *Maud in toto*: the phenomenon is so striking, its recurrence so persistent, as to demand explanation, and it is tempting to suspect that he found the experience both exciting and therapeutic. Ricks's description of the poem as 'audacious exorcism'[102] probably hits the nail on the head, and there was a peculiar audacity, even ruthlessness, in Tennyson's quest for an audience. Among the many listeners over the years was the 21-year-old Swinburne at Farringford in 1858; Allingham heard it, also at Farringford, in 1865 and found the poet's inter-polated comments 'very amusing' ('That's wonderfully fine!' he would exclaim; 'that was very hard to read; could you have read it? I don't think so'); Jane Welsh Carlyle was, almost incredibly, treated to it no fewer than four times in a few weeks and observed that Tennyson 'seemed strangely excited' about the poem; Jane Harrison found the listener's role produced 'an anxious joy', for she was expected to prompt the reciter when his memory failed him. There is a reference to a very early reading, perhaps the first, in a letter dated 26 September 1855, and his last reading, described in Hallam's *Memoir*, was on 24 August 1892, about six weeks before his death; the habit or addiction clearly persisted over a period of 37 years.

Tennyson read other poems and to other listeners, and this is an appropriate point at which to say something about his readings in general and his vocal style in particular. Unlike Dickens he never read in public or for money. In 1862 he was offered £20,000 – a fortune – for a reading tour of America; he turned the offer down, though he was flattered when Henry Irving told him he would have made a fine actor (he had acted in undergraduate productions at Cambridge, his best role being Malvolio). He started reading his poems to his close friends quite early (Fitz's 1838 reference to his 'magic music' has been quoted earlier), and after his marriage the readings became a regular feature of Tennysonian hospitality. Those who listened for their supper were not always let off lightly: a reading of *Harold* in 1876 lasted two and a half hours and sent Gladstone to sleep (Mary Gladstone noted with significant emphasis that the poet read with great vigour and power and 'evident enjoyment to himself'). Usually, though, the programme was more varied: one menu consisted of an extract from *Maud*, the dialect poem 'Northern Farmer (Old Style)', 'The Spinster's Sweet-Arts' and the Wellington 'Ode' – a judicious mingling of grave and gay. While many were deeply appreciative of the privilege of hearing the uniquely authoritative rendering, a few were less impressed: Henry James, hearing 'Locksley Hall', 'failed to swoon away' and decided that Tennyson 'wasn't Tennysonian'.

Tennyson's voice was evidently an instrument of great range and power and his style of reading highly individual, even eccentric. Fitz speaks of him 'Mouthing out his hollow oes and aes [a phrase from Tennyson's own poem 'The Epic'], deep-chested music, this is something as A.T. reads, with a broad north country vowel . . . His voice, very deep and deep-chested, but rather murmuring than mouthing like the sound of a far sea or of a pine-wood'. The regional accent remained, for when he gave a reading at George Eliot's home in 1877 a guest commented that 'I had at first some little difficulty in accustoming myself to his very marked Northern dialect'. Many accounts suggest that his readings were strongly rhythmical, closer to chanting than reading. Bram Stoker referred to his voice as 'powerful and vibrant', adding that 'in his reading there was a wonderful sense of time. The lines seemed to swing with an elastic step – like a regiment marching'; Emily Ritchie said that 'the roll of his great voice acted sometimes almost like an incantation'; and James Knowles observed that 'it was not reading as usually understood, but intoning on a note, almost chanting, which I heard, and which brought the conviction that this was the proper vehicle for poetry as distinguished from prose'. H. M. Butler referred to 'his peculiar manner of reading, with its deep and often monotonous tones, varied with a sudden lift of the voice as if into the air, at the end of a sentence or a clause'. A less respectful comment comes from Edmund Gosse: 'He hangs sleepily over the syllables, in a rough monotonous murmur, sacrificing everything to quantity. Had I not known the poem well beforehand it would have been entirely unintelligible'.

Some of the accounts of his readings of particular poems suggest that a Tennysonian reading may have constituted a particular interpretation, like Elgar or Britten conducting his own music, and sometimes with an element of the unexpected. In reading the opening lines of the 'Ode on the Death of the Duke of Wellington' ('Bury the Great Duke/ With an empire's lamentation . . .') he 'lengthened out the vowel a in the words great and lamentation, and rolled out and lengthened the open oes in the words "To the noise of the mourning of a mighty nation"'. Fitz says of 'St Simeon Stylites': 'This is one of the Poems A.T. would read with grotesque Grimness, especially at such passages as "Coughs, Aches, Stitches, etc.", laughing aloud at times'. And Wilfrid Ward noted that 'Vastness' had, 'as he first read it to me, two distinct voices – the last line being placed in the mouth of a separate speaker who answers the rest of the poem'. Such accounts make intelligible Tennyson's comment on his 'Boädicea', an experiment in an unfamiliar metre, that 'I cannot publish her yet, perhaps never, for who can read her except myself?' as well as Palgrave's valedictory remark after Tennyson's death that 'something of their music, some part of their very essence, has passed with the Maker'.[103]

Despite the critical attacks, *Maud* had some distinguished admirers, including Browning and Ruskin, and sold well. Its success encouraged Tennyson to proceed to the purchase of Farringford in April 1856, making him at 46 a homeowner for the first time. He had not, indeed, had a permanent home since the departure from Somersby. Observing that he now had 'the income of a rich man', Martin adds severely that it was 'a fact that he carefully concealed'.[104] It is true that an annual income of £2,000 or more was wealth by the standards of the day, but it should not be forgotten that, like any self-employed man, Tennyson must have been (and might reasonably have been) conscious of the uncertainty of his future earnings: the income of a poet, even a Laureate, may be subject to violent fluctuations, and if he were to die he would leave his wife and children with very little capital.

He was, moreover, a generous host, and the circle of friendships widened considerably now that he had a home of his own. It was a circle by no means confined to fellow authors, for in addition to poets such as Clough, Patmore and Swinburne it came to include (among many others) the artists Millais, Watts and Holman Hunt; the composer Sullivan; Grove the musicologist; Jenny Lind the singer; Ellen Terry the actress; Layard the archaeologist; Jowett the classical scholar and Master of Balliol; Bradley and Benson the public-school headmasters (the former subsequently

*48 Photograph by James Mudd, taken when Tennyson visited Manchester at the end of July 1857. The Tennysons attended the opening by the Queen of an art exhibition; also present was Nathaniel Hawthorne, who recorded his impression of Tennyson and of his companion Thomas Woolner: the black-bearded, black-hatted, black-coated Tennyson had 'nothing white about him except the collar of his shirt, which methought might have been clean the day before . . . He might well enough pass for a madman at any time, there being a wildness in his aspect, which doubtless might readily pass from quietude to frenzy'. During this visit the Tennysons also heard Dickens read* A Christmas Carol *at the Free Trade Hall.*

Dean of Westminster, the latter Archbishop of Canterbury); Weld the historian; Owen the zoologist; Lear the artist and nonsense poet; Dodgson, alias Carroll, don, mathematician and author; Palgrave, a civil servant for whose *Golden Treasury* (1861) Tennyson made numerous suggestions; not to mention aristocrats such as the Duke of Argyll and the Duchess of Sutherland, and famous hostesses such as Lady Ashburton. Three of his neighbours became close friends: Sir John Simeon, MP, Catholic convert and country gentleman; Julia Margaret Cameron, the pioneering

*49 Benjamin Jowett, the Greek scholar and (from 1870) Master of Balliol College, Oxford: photograph by Julia Margaret Cameron. Tennyson met Jowett in June 1855 when he went to Oxford to receive the honorary degree of Doctor of Civil Law, and Jowett became a frequent visitor to Farringford. When Jowett, having heard Tennyson read a new poem on a later visit to Oxford, advised him not to publish it, Tennyson remarked, 'If it comes to that, Master, the sherry you gave us at luncheon was beastly.'*

photographer; and W. G. Ward, theologian and, like Simeon, a Roman Catholic. This is only a very selective list of Tennyson's friendships; most of them beat a path to Farringford and some stayed for weeks on end. In the spring of 1861, for instance, the Cloughs were there for six weeks, Jowett for a fortnight; then came the Franklin Lushingtons, Tennyson's brother Horatio and his family, and the Welds. Geographically isolated though it was, Farringford was no ivory tower, and Tennyson had to cultivate a strict routine to get any work done at all. It says much for his

50 A page from Emily Tennyson's journal (September 1855). The first entry refers to a visit to Farringford by W. F. Pollock, lawyer and man of letters, and his wife; they did not escape without a reading of Maud. The last entry on this page notes that F. T. Palgrave was leaving after a ten-day visit.

dedication to his art that, though he could have afforded in his later years to lead a life of dignified leisure, he never retired from his occupation as poet.

His old friend Fitz records a glimpse of him in London in May 1857, 'bearded, and seeming very well but staying at a great House in Kensington with which I won't meddle'.[105] As this suggests, Fitz was sensitive to the changes taking place in the other's life: while he himself, indifferent to his aristocratic connections and his money, was sinking into a dim provincial existence, Alfred was moving in grander circles and apparently not disliking it. Even royalty, as well as being neighbours, were among the visitors to Farringford: while the Tennysons were still moving in their belongings, the Prince Consort dropped in, and later Tennyson was to visit Osborne House, sometimes with his family.

It was not a lifestyle that anyone would have predicted even ten years earlier. He had found new responsibilities (as a father, for instance, concerned about his sons' childish ailments and later their education) and new roles (as neighbour, host and public figure) that gave his life a new centre of gravity. Without his marriage to Emily his life after 1850 must have been entirely different and might well have been much shorter. Too much personal contentment may do no good to a creative artist, but there is a short answer to the anti-Emily argument that urges that without domestication he might have produced more exciting and experimental work in his later decades. Nobody can with certainty say that this would or would not have happened, and in any case there is nothing surprising about a writer becoming more sedate and conventional in his later years (many who are not writers do exactly the same), but it is surely undeniable that without marriage he might have had no creative future and possibly no future of any kind. The second half of his life was to be busier but less crisis-ridden than the first; it was hardly less productive, and it must have been immeasurably happier.

# ⇒ 3 ⇐
# THE
# MAKING
# OF THE
# LEGEND

T O BRING TENNYSON'S LIFE story to a rapid conclusion by declaring that Alfred and Emily lived happily ever after would be to leave out of account two major elements: the poems and the legend. He went on writing to the end, and some of his best poems, especially short poems, belong to his last years. And the legend grew rapidly quite soon after the move to Farringford and became firmly established in the last thirty years of his life. Partly, of course, it flourished because, like Victoria, he lasted so long: while some of his readers grew old along with him, younger and even middle-aged readers of his later volumes would have been unable to remember a time when he had not been the dominant figure in English poetry. If he had died at the same age as, say, Byron, there would have been no *Princess*, no *In*

*51 Tennyson with his wife and sons
in the garden at Farringford:
photograph by O. G. Rejlander, c. 1863.*

*Memoriam*, no *Maud*, no *Idylls of the King*, no 'Enoch Arden' . . . – and the legend itself would have taken a very different, and surely a less potent, form.

To become a legend in one's lifetime had its drawbacks, and very soon after the Tennysons settled at Farringford summer tourists became a worse nuisance than summer flies. Responsible for this was the growth of tourism as the railway network spread and the growth of Tennyson's own readership and popular and commercial success. His sales became, by present-day standards for poetry, phenomenal. When Moxon published an illustrated edition of his poems in 1857, the print run was 10,000. The *Idylls of the King* brought in over £4,500 in royalties in the year after publication (later the *Enoch Arden* volume was to do substantially better). He could earn a respectable sum for a single poem: *Macmillan's Magazine* paid £300 for 'Sea Dreams' (published January 1860), and later *Good Words* paid £700, or nearly £10 per very short line, for 'The Victim'. When 'Tithonus' appeared in the second issue of the *Cornhill* in February 1860, Thackeray's magazine sold 75,000 copies.

But some of the large audience implied by these figures wanted to see the great man with their own eyes, and some had scant respect for privacy or private property. It was not to be many years before the Tennysons began to think seriously about a second home, to enable them to escape from Farringford during the summer season, which from soon after the mid-century brought shoals of visitors to what had at first seemed as magically secluded as Prospero's island.

As it turned out, the move to the Isle of Wight was hardly a canny one for a lover of

*52 Letter from Tennyson to his son Hallam, conjecturally dated 29 April 1857. At this time Hallam was four years old and Tennyson had left Farringford for a visit of several weeks to London, where he visited his dentist, stayed at Little Holland House, and saw many friends, including FitzGerald, Spedding, Patmore, Holman Hunt, Henry Hallam, and the Camerons.*

seclusion. In 1853 the Farringford estate had still seemed isolated – the maidservants wept when they discovered how far from the world they had come – and the views were still unspoilt. Tennyson, too, found its loneliness irksome at times: 'We have hardly seen a human face since we came here except the members of our household,' he complained in April 1854.[106] The house itself, built at the turn of the century, had soon afterwards been enlarged in the style of the period with Gothic battlements, mullioned windows, and an artificial ruin. The estate had medieval origins, and the very name could be traced back to a fourteenth-century Walter de Farringford. When the Tennysons arrived there was still no railway on the island, and the eight-mile crossing from the mainland often had to be made by rowing-boat; when visitors did come they had to walk from Yarmouth, three and a half miles distant, while a donkey-cart brought up their luggage.

Changes came quickly, however. Osborne House had been constructed to the Prince Consort's designs in 1845–51 and 'thanks largely to Osborne, [the Isle of Wight] rose to be a favourite place for affluent English families to spend seaside holidays'.[107] Dickens took his family there in 1849, and later sent the Lammles (in *Our Mutual Friend*) there for their ill-starred honeymoon. Fashions in holiday resorts, as in other matters, filtered down the social scale, and where royalty went the well-to-do followed and the common tripper or 'Cockney' came after. Actually the island's popularity had begun a generation earlier – the census return of 1831 had reported a 'continual influx of strangers . . . capitalists, bankers, professional and other educated men'[108] – but it was in the generation from about 1840 that modern tourism really got into its stride. Thomas Cook inaugurated a quiet revolution by organising a temperance outing from Leicester to Loughborough in 1841; the phrase 'excursion train' (first used in a literary context by Thackeray) dates ominously from 1850; even more ominously the map of the Isle of Wight partially reproduced as Plate 45 and dated 1860 is titled 'Stanford's Tourist Map'.

By 1862, if not earlier, Tennyson was chafing at the 'cockneyism of this place': the idyll was turning sour. Walter White's journal notes that on 20 November 1864 he

*53 Tennyson with his sons Hallam (left) and Lionel: photograph by O. G. Rejlander, c. 1862.*

'talked about the encroachment of buildings around Far[r]ingford, and the villas and hotel that are to be built at Alum Bay'.[109] In that year the Tennysons took their summer holiday in France to escape the tourists at home; later in the year Emily persuaded her husband that they should find a summer residence. Her own preference was for Surrey, where she had lived for a time before her marriage. Tennyson was hard to please, and it was only in 1867 that he purchased a site and

*54 Sketch of Aldworth by Emily Tennyson.*

engaged his friend Knowles to design a house. He was, as he told Palgrave on 23 March, 'flying from the Cockneys'.[110]

Aldworth House (now in private hands) lies just south of the Surrey–Sussex border, a few miles southeast of Haslemere and close to Black Down (National Trust). In the 1860s the area was still difficult of access, as Tennyson's old friend Milnes, now Lord Houghton, somewhat sharply observed in a letter to his wife after

*55 Engraving of Aldworth reproduced in* The Leisure Hour *(1874). Walter White described it as 'a palatial-looking house on a small scale'.*

a visit in 1871: 'He has built himself a very handsome and commodious house in a most inaccessible site, with every comfort he can require, and every discomfort to all who approach him. What can be more poetical?'[111] For its owner the isolation of 'a house 800 feet above the sea – no roads and no post'[112] was one of its attractions, though he also enjoyed its unaccustomed amenities and at first took 'three baths a day'.[113] It was, perhaps, grander than he might have wished: that, at least, is what he told a neighbour, James Mangles, who became a friend. After their first meeting in August 1870, Mangles wrote in his diary (discovered in 1961 and published in 1984): 'The view was magnificent; but he missed, he said, the country sounds, whetting of scythes, reapers' songs, & sheep & cattle – and the birds, he said, don't seem to care to come so high. "This fellow," pointing to the architect, "makes me have all this. I should be contented with something much simpler"'.[114] Some may find his protestation less than wholly convincing.

Long before this Tennyson was a public figure and was moving in social circles considerably higher than the birds. During a visit to London in May 1857 he wrote to Emily: 'The second day after my arrival much to my disgust seven papers announced my arrival, "from his seat Farringford, Freshwater, I.W."'.[115] Perhaps there was a mite of self-satisfaction mingled with the 'disgust'. Another letter told her that he had spent the morning 'with the Duke and Duchess of Argyll, both amazingly kind'.[116] The following year, in London again, he was, according to William Michael Rossetti, 'inevitably "the observed of all observers"'.[117] His fame, too, was spreading abroad: in Norway the same summer 'a Norwegian introduced himself at the hotel, and began to spout my own verses to me'.[118] Among innumerable fan letters came one in 1860 from the Prince Consort, asking him to sign a copy of his *Idylls*. But what was gratifying from royalty could be tiresome from lesser mortals, and by 1865 Tennyson was railing at one of the penalties of his great fame, 'our worse than Egyptian plague of letters, books, MSS etc. not from England alone but from the colonies, U.S., even France, Italy, Germany – nay Liberia and the negroes . . .'. Allingham's diary confirms this with a reference to 'Letters for Tennyson from Poets sending specimens of their work, and autograph seekers'.[119] It seems that every bad poet who had published a slim volume at his own expense promptly dispatched it to the Poet Laureate.

The death of Albert in December 1861 had the immediate effect of reminding him of his feelings when Hallam died. Its long-term effect was to bring him into a closer

*56 Letter from the Prince Consort to Tennyson (17 May 1860), asking him to autograph his copy of* Idylls of the King. *The Prince's death in the following year led Tennyson to compose a prefatory dedication for a new edition of the* Idylls.

relationship with the Queen. In February 1862, he sent her a copy of a new edition of the *Idylls of the King* with an added dedication 'To the Prince Consort'; its concluding line had been quoted earlier in the month in Lord Dufferin's parliamentary eulogy of the dead Prince. Victoria's response to Tennyson's gesture was to indicate that she would like to see him the next time she was at Osborne, and after enquiries as to proper behaviour in the royal presence he presented himself there on 14 April and was gratifyingly informed by the Queen that after the Bible her main solace in her grief was *In Memoriam*. This was apparently his first audience; the acquaintance ripened and a correspondence ensued. (Their relationship may be traced in detail in Hope Dyson & Charles Tennyson's *Dear and Honoured Lady* [1969].) The most important link between them was the shared experience of bereavement, and it seems likely that to some extent the Queen mentally rewrote *In Memoriam* with Albert as hero.

*57 Inscription by Queen Victoria in a copy of* The Principal Speeches and Addresses of His Royal Highness the Prince Consort. With an introduction giving some outline of his character *(1862), presented to Tennyson. The Poet Laureate had paid his first visit to the Queen on 14 April 1862, exactly four months after the Prince's death; on that occasion she had told him that, after the Bible,* In Memoriam *was her principal source of comfort and that the description of Hallam reminded her of the Prince. 'When rumours of his visit to the Queen and of their correspondence became current, national curiosity began to display an insistence which seriously embarrassed and irritated [Tennyson]' (Sir Charles Tennyson).*

In 1873 Tennyson visited Windsor by royal invitation and was shown the Prince Consort's tomb: 'The Queen took me into the building and explained everything'.[120] A family visit to Osborne in 1863 is charmingly described by the ten-year-old Hallam, who had been carefully coached in courtly etiquette: 'You must always say "Mam" when in her Majesty's presence. You must stand until the Queen asks you to sit down. Her Majesty does not *often* tell you to sit down'.[121]

The laureate duties were not unduly burdensome, though he did not always escape the chore of penning verses to celebrate a royal occasion. In 1858 he wrote two extra stanzas for the National Anthem to be sung at the Princess Royal's wedding: 'As to my stanzas,' he told the Duchess of Argyll, I do not pique myself upon them: they are neither much better nor worse than the rest of that loyal confection'.[122]

The four poems written in 1856–9 and published in July 1859 as *Idylls of the King*

*59 Photograph taken by W. Jeffrey on 6 May 1862.*

are only part of an enterprise that occupied Tennyson on and off for over half a century. His poetic exploration and exploitation of the then relatively unfamiliar Arthurian material was to involve him in extensive research. It began with 'The Lady of Shalott'; *Morte d'Arthur*, written in 1833–4 (but not published until 1842), was part of his response to the death of that other Arthur and established the form of blank-verse narrative that was to be followed throughout. A generation later, the dedication written soon after the Prince Consort's death and published in 1862 linked the legendary king with the modern prince ('And indeed he seemed to me/ Scarce other than my king's ideal knight . . .'), extended the parallel between the fictional character and those who had been part of Tennyson's own life, prompted Swinburne to suggest that the poems might have been described as a Morte d'Albert.

The group of poems, constituting in the end a kind of historical novel in verse, continued to grow for another generation. *The Holy Grail and Other Poems* (1869)

*58 Lionel (left) and Hallam
Tennyson: photograph by
O. G. Rejlander, c. 1863.*

*60 Tennyson's summer-house in the grounds of Farringford, 'in which "Enoch Arden" was written': engraving by W. Biscombe Gardner, reproduced in an article by Grant Allen in the* English Illustrated Magazine *in 1892.*

provided, among other things, a frame in the shape of 'The Coming of Arthur' and 'The Passing of Arthur', the latter formed by adding 169 lines to the beginning and 29 to the end of the old *Morte d'Arthur*. It was in the same year that Tennyson gave the title *The Round Table* to the collection of poems. 'Gareth and Lynette' appeared in 1872, 'Balin and Balan', composed in 1872–4, not until 1885. All told, the series comprises ten poems with the 'Coming' and 'Passing' as prologue and epilogue, and runs to well over 10,000 lines.

Its contemporary fame marked a split between the popular and the critical readerships: as Walter Bagehot shrewdly noted, the general public were more enthusiastic than 'Mr Tennyson's straiter disciples'. Frederic Harrison described it as 'a fierce lusty epic . . . emasculated into a moral lesson for an academy of young ladies', and G. M. Hopkins labelled it 'Charades from the Middle Ages'. But in a period when the long narrative poem could still command a large popular audience it was admired by countless less distinguished readers.

Commercially, the *Idylls* did well and *Enoch Arden and Other Poems* (1864) even better: 17,000 copies of the latter were sold on the day of publication, and the first impression of 60,000 copies was sold out by the end of the year. 'It was,' writes Jump, 'an extraordinarily popular volume, perhaps more so than any other by its author.'[123] In *Tennyson and his Publishers* (1979) June Steffensen Hagen reproduces a sheet of paper showing (in Emily Tennyson's handwriting) Tennyson's half-yearly income from royalties for the six years from the end of 1859. The second half of that year was a good period (£3,536.11.2), thanks to the *Idylls*, but this sum was almost doubled in the second half of 1864 (£6,664.4.2). Though the title poem, 'Enoch Arden', is now unfashionable – partly, perhaps, on account of our own age's inability to deal with pathos – it immediately won a place in the hearts of mid-Victorian readers at home and abroad. Sir Charles Tennyson goes so far as to nominate it 'the most popular poem [Tennyson] ever wrote'; certainly it won an immense and devoted public. At least 28 translations appeared, it was adapted for the stage, and even after the turn of the century it became the subject of several silent film versions. The quality of the response it evoked can be gauged from the language used by some of the reviewers: it was, said one, 'as holy as an angel's dream', while another urged that the story it told 'might . . . undulate in rippling cadences from Seraph tongues'. On one occasion when the poet read it aloud he judged it necessary to beseech his audience in advance not to go into hysterics.[124]

The same volume also contains another narrative poem, 'Aylmer's Field', as well as a number of memorable shorter pieces. Among these is 'Tithonus', an earlier and shorter version of which dates from 1833; 'Northern Farmer' (the subtitle 'Old Style'

*61 Photograph taken by Julia Margaret Cameron on 3 June 1869: Tennyson said it made him look like 'a dirty monk'.*

was added later); and 'In the Valley of Cauteretz', written in August 1861 on revisiting 'a valley in the Pyrenees where I had been with A.H.':

All along the valley, stream that flashest white,
Deepening thy voice with the deepening of the night,
All along the valley, where thy waters flow,
I walked with one I loved two and thirty years ago.
All along the valley, while I walked today,
The two and thirty years were a mist that rolls away;
For all along the valley, down thy rocky bed,
Thy living voice to me was as the voice of the dead,
And all along the valley, by rock and cave and tree,
The voice of the dead was a living voice to me.

The poem spans the years in ten lines and with remarkable economy of means, deriving much of its power from the reappearance of a few key phrases – an echo-chamber of a poem. (Tennyson, who cared about accuracy, was distressed later to find he had got the sum wrong: it was not 'two and thirty years ago' but 31 years since he had been there with Hallam.) As these examples suggest, Tennyson in his middle years was still drawing on the knowledge, the emotions and the poetic drafts of his youth.

The decade ended, as we have seen, with the publication of four more Idylls, as *The Holy Grail and Other Poems* (1869): Tennyson's serial poem, as Kathleen Tillotson calls it, was growing in bulk as well as in fame. It was at about this time that the *Saturday Review*, in hailing Tennyson as the supreme English poet of the age, predicted 'that he would be known to posterity "as the poet of Arthur"'.[125]

His fame in this period can hardly be exaggerated: 'Reviewers in the *Spectator* thought him "more likely than any living sovereign, and as likely as any living statesman, to give a name to the age" and hailed him as "our only great living poet"'.

His bust (by Woolner) had been placed in the library of Trinity College, 'said to be the first time that a living poet had been so honoured'. When he attended Dickens's funeral in 1870, the congregation in the Abbey pressed forward at the conclusion of the service to gain a glimpse of him. On a less stately level, the enterprising

*62 Tennyson welcomes Garibaldi to Farringford (*Illustrated London News, *23 April 1864). 'The Italian hero was the hero of England that spring,' but 'As reported by Tennyson, the conversation in the study was somewhat inconclusive. Both men spoke English but failed almost totally to understand each other . . . Things went better when they quoted Italian poetry to each other' (Martin). It was during this visit that Mrs Cameron, rushing up to Garibaldi, falling on her knees, and imploring him to come and have his photograph taken, was mistaken for a beggarwoman (the photograph was not taken).*

manufacturers of Cockles' Pills 'printed an entirely fictitious letter reading: "Dear Sir, Like most literary men I am subject to violent constipation, & your pills I find of the greatest possible comfort. Yrs A. Tennyson"'.[126]

In personal terms, he was now well past the age at which his father had died – for many men a significant and even ominous landmark – and had achieved happiness and stability, as well as wealth and fame, that may have been beyond the wildest dreams or most ardent yearnings of his tormented youth. He had two large houses, each with its own staff, as well as a flat in London; one of his sons (Lionel) was at Eton, the other at Marlborough. And he had a large circle of friends – though, like all who live long enough, he suffered the loss of some. In 1870 he was grieved by the death of his neighbour Sir John Simeon; 'In the Garden at Swainton' mourns him along with two who had died earlier, Arthur Hallam and Henry Lushington:

> Nightingales warbled without,
>   Within was weeping for thee:
> Shadows of three dead men
>   Walked in the walks with me,
> Shadows of three dead men and thou wast one of the three.

Lushington, a Trinity contemporary, fellow Apostle, and the dedicatee of *The Princess*, had died in 1855, Thackeray in 1863.

From time to time Tennyson continued to fret about his health, as he had always done; but the fact is that he had no serious illness until he was in his late seventies. The moroseness and misanthropy of his early years had given way to something approaching geniality: though he could still be *farouche* on occasions that may have lost nothing in the telling, it was an amiable eccentricity of the kind that seems proper and even necessary to a great man. Out walking with a child friend, for instance, 'He would always wear his great Spanish cloak and sombrero, which excited much interest. The real cause of this he never seemed to realize, for he would say to his little companion: "Child, your mother should dress you less conspicuously; people are staring at us"'.[127]

His later years were notably gregarious, and the list of his social engagements and encounters reads like a muster-roll of eminent Victorians and not a few distinguished

*63 Lionel Tennyson: photograph by Julia Margaret Cameron.*

foreign visitors. To take, almost at random, a single month in the summer of 1871: after receiving Turgenev as a guest at Aldworth, Tennyson went to London, saw (among others) Mark Pattison and G. F. Watts, and met Edmund Gosse and G. H. Lewes; the latter took him to meet George Eliot, and during the summer he saw the Leweses several times, treating George Eliot on one occasion to the inevitable recitation of *Maud*. He also saw the Gladstones, Fanny Kemble, Lord Houghton, and Clough's widow. There were 'seasons' in London, when he took a house for a period of weeks or months, and trips abroad, including climbing holidays with Hallam in the Swiss and Italian Alps and the Pyrenees. (He was haunting Cauteretz once more in September 1874.) Though now well into his sixties he showed no flagging of his physical energy: indeed he was in many respects leading a much more active life than in his youth. Nor did he tire easily in company, particularly if there was a chance to read his own poems: on 30 March 1877, when he read *Maud*

*64 Dawing of Tennyson by 'Ape' (Carlo Pellegrini), published in* Vanity Fair *on 22 July 1871 in the series 'Men of the Day'. (Pellegrini was an important influence on Max Beerbohm, whose well-known 'Mr Tennyson reading "In Memoriam" to his Sovereign' was included in his* The Poets' Corner *[1904].)*

and other poems to the assembled company at George Eliot's London home, The Priory, near Regent's Park, he had to be stopped by Hallam at midnight.

It was Emily who was to collapse through overwork in 1874. For years she had taken upon herself the huge burden of Tennyson's correspondence and, going beyond what many would have regarded as the call of duty, had felt a moral obligation to answer everyone (and they were legion) who wrote to ask the Bard for literary or ethical counsel. Tennyson made no secret of his dislike of letter-writing (his own letters, fewer than 2,000 of which survive, are mostly short), and there may have been a touch of selfishness, or at least thoughtlessness, in his allowing Emily to do so much for so long. For her part she seems to have seen her role as protective, but after nearly a quarter of a century the task proved too much for her. A little more ruthlessness in leaving letters from strangers unanswered might have saved her health, but she belonged to a generation that took Wordsworth's 'Ode to Duty' seriously, though we may consider her notion of duty misguided. Jowett certainly did so, for he warned her as early as 1861: 'It grieves me to see you who care for the most trifling wants of other people so helpless about yourself . . . Do not throw away your life in the performance of imaginary duties which are really un-important . . . It is not the letterwriting etc. but your life and presence that are the real good and blessing in the house'.[128] This good advice went unheeded, and her last words when she died in 1896 were to be of regret for duty only partially ful-filled: 'I might have done more'.[129] But it is impossible to judge her as harshly as she

66 This photograph of Tennyson by Julia Margaret Cameron was taken on 3 June 1869, shortly before he left for a walking holiday in Switzerland, and two months before his sixtieth birthday.

judged herself: Tennyson was lucky in his choice of a wife, and the transformation of the second half of his life by marriage was little short of miraculous.

The collapse came soon after their return from a holiday in France. The weather had been unseasonably cold, and Emily had remained in Tours with Lionel while Tennyson and Hallam went on to the Pyrenees. One consequence was that the journal she had begun in the year of her marriage came to an end. On 16 October

1874 Tennyson wrote to Palgrave: 'My wife I am sorry to say from overwork and over-letterwriting is still obliged to lie flat and must not exert herself in any one thing (the Doctor says) if she be to recover; and so a good deal of the work falls on me, who, you know, abhor letterwriting'.[130] Recovery was not rapid and was never complete. The following summer Tennyson described her to Browning as 'helpless and hori-

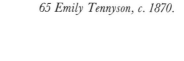

*65 Emily Tennyson, c. 1870.*

zontal' and unable to write or read, and told the Duchess of Argyll: 'I fear it will be a long time before she recovers her old self, and be able to write letters for five hours a-day, not that I shall ever let her do so again'.[131] The horizontality became a regular feature of her subsequent life and is referred to in many accounts of the Tennysons' later years: in 1880 Thomas Hardy, arriving for lunch with them in London, found her lying 'as if in a coffin'; though she rose to greet him she presided at the table in a

67 *Audrey, wife of Hallam Tennyson, from a painting by Briton Riviere.*

reclining position.[132] Allingham's diary for 1884 gives what must have been a characteristic glimpse: 'Lady Tennyson came down to dinner, very pale – spoke and was spoken to little, went upstairs again, almost carried by Hallam. A dear, almost angelic woman'.[133]

Her epistolary function was taken over by Hallam, who left Cambridge before completing his time there at the end of 1875: as he observes in his *Memoir*, after that date he 'remained at home as my father's secretary, a capacity in which there was much to be done'.[134] He continued in this capacity until his father's death: when he married Audrey Boyle in 1884 she simply moved into the Tennyson home, assisted Hallam in his duties, accompanied Tennyson on his daily walks, and in due course stood beside his deathbed. There were times, however, when even the youth and energy, not to mention the dedication, of Hallam and Audrey could not cope with the flood of fan mail, and in 1885, after the publication of *Tiresias and Other Poems*, Tennyson was obliged to announce in *The Times* (through his publisher) that he was 'wholly unable to answer the innumerable letters which he daily receives, nor can he undertake to return or criticise the manuscripts sent to him'.[135]

*68 Hallam Tennyson: serious, responsible, and seemingly mindful of the great responsibility of being his father's secretary and, eventually, his biographer.*

For a number of years from the mid-1870s Tennyson devoted much time and effort to his poetic dramas. It was a late and somewhat unexpected change of direction in his career, but he had always venerated Shakespeare and there may have been an element of striving to emulate the highest (he had, after all, attempted a modern epic in his *Idylls*). In any case, other Victorian poets, like the Romantics before them, had had similar ambitions. He can hardly have been driven on by hopes of profit, for a contract with his new publisher, Henry King, in 1873 had guaranteed him an income of £5,000 a year for the next five years, excluding royalties on any new works. Little read and less performed today, the plays cannot be said to have been a resounding success even in their own time, and there are signs that Tennyson simply knew too little about the practical conditions of the theatre to make a successful dramatist.

*Queen Mary*, begun in the spring of 1874, was published in the following year and produced at the Lyceum Theatre on 18 April 1876 but ran for only five weeks, and then only in an abbreviated form. Tennyson, however, quickly immersed himself in the composition of *Harold*, dedicated to Bulwer-Lytton's son (presumably in an attempt to mend the old quarrel). It was completed in time to be read in its entirety to the Gladstone family when Tennyson and Hallam visited Hawarden in October. The diary of Mary Gladstone, one of the Prime Minister's daughters, already cited, contains some interesting thumbnail sketches: Tennyson 'snubbed me once or twice, but was afterwards very amiable. He is exactly like Shakespeare to look at . . . [Hallam] worships his Father and sits adoring'. During the reading Hallam was 'now and then referred to by his father and ha[d] to fill in a word or passage, actually knowing it all by heart'.[136]

Soon *Harold* was in print and *Becket* begun. The latter, however, did not appear until the end of 1884; in the theatre it was to prove more successful than its predecessors, having a particularly good run at the Lyceum with Henry Irving in the title role in the year after Tennyson's death. A one-act play, *The Falcon*, was produced in 1879 and a two-act play *The Cup* ran for four months in 1881, partly perhaps because the cast was headed by Irving and Ellen Terry.

An important new friendship, formed in the early 1870s and briefly mentioned a little earlier, was with W. G. Ward, who had settled at Freshwater. Ward had been an Oxford don who, falling under the influence of the Tractarians, lost his fellowship and became a Roman Catholic. In 1870 he had become President of the Metaphysical Society, in the foundation of which Tennyson had been active. At the Society's first formal meeting on 2 June 1869 Tennyson's poem 'The Higher Pantheism' had been read aloud. Hallam later described the object of the Society: 'that those who were ranged on the side of faith should meet those who were ranged on the side of unfaith, and freely interchange their views'.[137] Among its early members were leading intellectuals such as T. H. Huxley, R. H. Hutton, J. A. Froude, Frederic Harrison, Henry Sidgwick, Mark Pattison and Walter Bagehot, as well as Gladstone and Cardinal Manning. Tennyson's involvement indicates that he naturally consorted with the advanced thinkers of his day, unbelievers as well as those representing various complexions of orthodoxy, and that he conceived his role as contributing to the harmonising of the new science with traditional faith.

It was in a sense a continuation of the public role that had been begun with the publication of *In Memoriam*, but it also suggests that even in his later years his mind was open to new arguments and new evidence. He had always been interested in science, and the programme of study he drew up, no doubt for therapeutic purposes, after Hallam's death included chemistry, botany, electricity, mechanics and animal physiology as well as history and theology. He read Sir Charles Lyell's profoundly influential *Principles of Geology* (1830–33) in 1837, and later read the popular *Vestiges of Creation* (1844) by Robert Chambers. As Elaine Jordan has pointed out, his Trinity tutor William Whewell 'played a major part in revising natural theology towards an understanding of development'. His own role was to be that of a populariser: 'The significance of [his] work in relation to science is not a matter of the knowledge shown about this or that phenomenon or hypothesis, but of the imaginative negotiation of changes of ideas about the world and time'. Writers on science such as Huxley and Tyndall were prompt to quote him and glad to draw on the prestige and moral authority of his name; at the same time they 'testified to the depth and accuracy of his scientific understanding'.[138] There is no need to be patronising (as W. H. Auden notoriously was, yielding too easily to the seductions of an antithesis[139]) about

Tennyson's intellectual equipment, though he was concerned less with the content of the new science than with its emotional and spiritual implications.

Relevant passages from *In Memoriam* and *Maud* have already been cited. In 'Lucretius', written in the 1860s, he speaks of 'momentary man':

> And even his bones long laid within the grave,
> The very sides of the grave itself shall pass,
> Vanishing, atom and void, atom and void,
> Into the unseen for ever . . .
>
> (lines 255–8)

And near the end of *In Memoriam*:

> There rolls the deep where grew the tree.
> O earth, what changes hast thou seen!
> There, where the long street roars, hath been
> The stillness of the central sea.
>
> (CXXIII)

Such passages convey a vertiginous sense of solid reality slipping away as unthought-of vistas of time are opened up. It was a sense that Tennyson's was the very first generation to experience.

For the Victorians, space opened up as well as time. Among Tennyson's numerous scientist-friends were the astronomers Sir John Herschel and Charles Pritchard, and astronomy had always held a special interest for him. As a boy he is reputed to have advised his brother Frederick to deal with social self-consciousness by thinking of 'Herschel's great star-patches' (this was Sir William Herschel, discoverer of Uranus and father of his friend). Half a century later James Mangles testified to his continuing fascination with the revealed wonders of the heavens: 'Spoke of Astronomy, took out his watch, pointed to the second hand. "At every tick, the Earth & Sirius are flying 40 miles asunder"'. Though Tennyson (or Mangles) has not got this figure quite right – contemporary scientific belief put it at 29 miles per second, later revised to 20 – the significant point is that he had apparently encountered the fact in the *Monthly Notices of the Royal Astronomical Society* (his copy is in the Tennyson Research Centre) only two years earlier. It was not every Victorian poet's idea of required reading.

His scientific interests later came to embrace psychology and the paranormal. The same entry in Mangles' diary notes that in the course of conversation he

> Returned to spiritualism – very curious about it – told several anecdotes. Had himself mesmerised, & the patient could prophesy his coming & feel his approach. Believed that a fluid passed from one to the other. Had heard that only force in Nature was Will-force. Might be – would like to know more about it.[140]

Like Dickens, he evidently had not only an intellectual interest in 'mesmerism' but decided gifts as a hypnotist; this was no new fad, for almost twenty years earlier he had used his mesmeric powers therapeutically at Malvern. On another occasion he 'set [Emily] right by mesmerising' after she had suffered pain and sleeplessness for nine days.[141]

In 1882 he was one of the founder members of the Society for Psychical Research, and the longing for assurance of personal immortality is one of the links between his scientific interests and his religious beliefs. He was not much of a churchgoer, perhaps not even a Christian in the strictest sense. Mary Gladstone, recording a breakfast-table conversation at Hawarden in 1876 on 'eternal punishment (in which T. firmly disbelieves), the immortality of the soul, and prayer', noted: 'T. does not appear to be much of a Christian, and I suspect is no theologian, but very really religious'.[142] But the idea of a Godless universe, and of death as total extinction, appalled him: as he told Allingham on 3 November 1872, '"If I ceased to believe in any chance of another life, and of a great Personality somewhere in the Universe, I should not care a pin for anything. People must have some religion"'.[143] Even more emphatically, in conversation with the Queen in 1883, he 'spoke with horror of the unbelievers and philosophers who would make one believe that there was no other world, no immortality', and sovereign and poet 'agreed that were such a thing possible, God, who is love, would be far more cruel than any human being'.[144] At times there was something pathetically desperate about his quest for reassurance: 'he described how he questioned every person whom he thought likely to be able to help him, and would in his walks and travels seek out the poor old men and women in the fields and cottages to ask them about their views on death and the future life'.[145] An essential element in his conception of immortality was the survival of personality: as he declared in 1869, '". . . there are moments when the flesh is nothing to me, when I feel and know the flesh to be the vision, God and the Spiritual the only real and true. Depend upon it, the Spiritual *is* the real: it belongs to one more than the hand and the foot. You may tell me that my hand and my foot are only imaginary symbols of my existence, I could believe you; but you never, never can convince me that the *I* is not an eternal Reality, and that the Spiritual is not the true and real part of me"'.[146] A short poem of the previous year, 'Wages', while apparently rejecting traditional notions of heaven, insists that without confidence in the survival of what is best in the individual, life is meaningless and unendurable:

> The wages of sin is death: if the wages of Virtue be dust,
>     Would she have heart to endure for the life of the worm and the fly?
> She desires no isles of the blest, no quiet seats of the just,
>     To rest in a golden grove, or to bask in a summer sky:
> Give her the wages of going on, and not to die.

But while he '*felt* the reality of the spirit world "a great ocean pressing round us on every side, and only leaking in by a few chinks"',[147] the poet who had won the gratitude of thousands for reconciling 'the larger hope' with the threats posed by the new science was not immune from doubt and even despair. Sir Frederick Pollock's jest that the Metaphysical Society had been founded 'for the purpose of convincing Tennyson of the immortality of the soul' had a serious side to it.[148] One of the most touching anecdotes of his later years shows him turning in desperation to a child (Sophia Palmer, daughter of Lord Selborne):

'Tell me,' he said to Sophia one day, 'if you saw your father's and mother's bones, skeletons, lying in the grave, saw their bodies over-mastered by corruption, would it over-master you? Would you feel they were there? That that was all? Think! just their bones – corruption! Would you?' Sophia, after some self-questioning, replied that she was certain that she would not be over-mastered – she would feel that what she saw was not those she loved, that they were still alive, more so than before. 'You are sure?' he pressed her; and on her repeating her assurance, 'Ah well!' he said, with rather pathetic relief, 'Yes, I too hold it so. I have tried to say it – to show it – that the body is the husk – the shell. But at times these new lights, this science wearies and perplexes me; yet I know they cannot reach, cannot explain . . .'[149]

Like anyone else growing old, Tennyson found as the years passed that his circle of family and friends provided occasions for both joy and sorrow. Lionel married in February 1878 and Tennyson's first grandchild was born before the end of the year and christened Alfred Browning Stanley. A second son, Charles Bruce (later Sir Charles), was born in the following year and was to become one of his grandfather's best biographers and to maintain the family tradition of longevity by surviving until 1978. Lionel's wedding took place in Westminster Abbey and was one of the social events of the year: F. W. Farrar, whose *Eric, or Little by Little* had made him famous twenty years earlier and who, as a Canon of Westminster, presumably knew what he

*69 Lionel Tennyson: the beautiful child photographed by Mrs Cameron grew into a handsome Old Etonian who contracted 'jungle fever' while hunting in Assam and died, aged thirty-two, as the homeward-bound ship was passing up the Red Sea.*

was talking about, considered that 'the assemblage of notabilities was one of the most remarkable which I have ever witnessed'.[150] Socially Tennyson had come a long way since his own almost inaudibly quiet wedding in an obscure village church. Hallam and Audrey, whose marriage in 1884 has already been mentioned, gave Tennyson two more grandsons (a third son was born in 1896, after his death).

But the naming of Hallam's firstborn, Lionel, in 1889, commemorated a family tragedy, for the older Lionel did not live to enjoy his happy family life for long. In connection with his duties at the India Office he travelled to India, contracted 'jungle fever', lay seriously ill for some time, and died in the Red Sea on the way home in April 1886. Tennyson's poem 'To the Marquis of Dufferin and Ava' (the addressee was Governor-General of India, Lionel's host, and a friend of the poet) was written two or three years later and revealingly uses the *In Memoriam* stanza:

*70 The photographer photographed: Julia Margaret Cameron, by her brother-in-law Lord Somers (1862). The Camerons settled at 'Dimbola', within walking distance of Farringford, in 1860, and Julia took up photography in 1863. According to Agnes Weld, she was 'almost the only woman outside [Tennyson's] relations whom he called by her Christian name, and who called him by his'.*

> Not there to bid my boy farewell,
> When That within the coffin fell,
> Fell – and flash'd into the Red Sea,
>
> Beneath a hard Arabian moon
> And alien stars. To question, why
> The sons before the fathers die,
> Not mine! . . .
>
> (lines 42–8)

Charles Turner, Tennyson's favourite brother, had died in 1879 and other deaths, less close but close enough to cause grief, followed. Louisa, Charles's widow, died less than a month after her husband, and Julia Margaret Cameron,

71 *Tennyson's friend James Spedding (left), with F. D. Maurice: photograph by O. G. Rejlander (c. 1859).*

close friend as well as near neighbour, had died earlier in the year. 1881 saw the deaths of Carlyle, Spedding and Stanley, the next year that of Ward. Fitz died in 1883: he and Tennyson had grown apart – not at all an unfamiliar phenomenon with early friendships, and if any blame is to be attached it should probably be shared. Martin, who is Fitz's biographer as well as Tennyson's, shrewdly suspects that there was in Fitz 'a perverse imp stirring him to say the very things he knew would irritate'[151] his friend, genuine though his affection was. But there had been a happy last meeting and there was, for us, a happy poetic outcome. In 1876, travelling in East Anglia with Hallam, Tennyson called on Fitz without warning at his home in Wood-bridge, Suffolk. As Fitz told a friend a few days later, 'immediately it was as if we had parted only twenty days instead of twenty years, with our old Jokes, Banter, Comparisons of Taste, etc.'.[152] Nearly seven years later Tennyson commemo-rated the visit in a poem that Ricks has justly described as 'one of the finest of [his] epistles'.[153] Quite why he should have done so at this time is not clear, but it turned out to have a melan-choly aptness, for a day or two later he heard that Fitz was dead. In the *Tiresias* volume of 1885 'To E. FitzGerald' stands first, while a 32-line pendant to the title poem mourns his friend's death. Noting that 'To E. FitzGerald'

72 These verses are contained in a letter dated 8 September 1885 and written by Edward Lear to Hallam Tennyson. Tennyson met Lear through Edmund Lushington, and Lear became a frequent visitor to Farringford. He later named his house in San Remo 'Villa Tennyson'. Another letter written at about the same time has similar drawings at the end with the labels 'Edward Lear aet 73.1/2' and 'His cat Foss, aet 16'.

consists of a single 56-line sentence, Ricks bestows the highest praise on its 'dignity' and 'affectionate tact': the poem 'breathes friendship' and is a moral as much as a stylistic achievement.[154] It belongs in fact to a group of poems of Tennyson's later years that commemorate long friendships ('To Mary Boyle' is a shorter but no less exquisite example) and in which Tennyson has attained an extraordinary poise, relaxed yet perfectly controlled, deeply felt but aloof from the emotional turmoil that can make his earlier work anguished and tormented. Such

155

*73 From a lithograph of a drawing by F. Sandys (1884).*

poems make Tennyson one of the best of our geriatric poets, though unlike Hardy or Yeats he celebrates longevity, his own and others'.

There are many images, verbal as well as visual, of Tennyson as he grew older, for of the countless number who met him a fair proportion sooner or later set down in private or public contexts their impressions or recollections. Inevitably, just as many of the visual representations are carefully posed studio portraits, some of these descriptions have a formal quality that makes one wonder whether the observers were seeing what they expected to see; but there are also some unexpected glimpses. In 1865 A. J. Munby, minor poet and civil servant, was crossing from the Isle of Wight to the mainland and spotted the great man:

. . . [he] wore old careless dress, tall wideawake, camlet [waterproof] cloak, loose blue trousers, frock coat and open shirt front – no gloves. Long wild curling hair: beard thin on cheeks, full round wide lips and chin. Complexion sallow, finely cut aquiline nose, veined: mouth grave and subtle in expression, face deeply lined: eyes hidden by blue spectacles. Voice deep and slow: gait stooping and heavy, almost aged. I watched him talking with a fat parson: round him other parsons, tourists, sailors; and his face supreme in manliness and mental power.[155]

The subtext of this reverential portrait suggests that here was a man one would look at twice on account of the unconventionality of his appearance, but there is a characteristic emphasis on Tennyson's immediately apparent difference from the ordinary run of men. Some poets look like bankers, publishers or insurance executives (and some are), but Tennyson never looked like anything other than a poet.

The quality of his physical presence, and especially his head and profile, in terms of a work of art is another recurring theme. The Quaker diarist Caroline Fox met him when he was touring Cornwall in 1860 and found him 'a grand specimen of a man, with a magnificent head set on his shoulders like the capital of a mighty pillar. His hair is long and wavy and covers a massy head. He wears a beard and a moustache, which one begrudges as hiding so much of that firm, powerful, but finely-chiselled mouth . . . I can quite understand Samuel Laurence calling it the best balance of head he had ever seen'. Another diarist, Marian Bradley, wife of the headmaster of Marlborough College, was also struck by that magnificent head: 'His glorious profile as he sat in the high back chair reading was most striking, there are lines furrowed deeper and deeper from brow to chin. There is a look in his face like a brightly burning light, like an inward fire consuming his life'. In 1866 a Haslemere neighbour, Anne Gilchrist, was one of several who found he looked older than she had expected (he was in fact still in his fifties): 'the portraits one was early familiar with have stood still in one's mind as the image to be associated with that great name'. But, she added, 'he is to my thinking far nobler looking now; every inch a king; features are massive, eyes very grave and penetrating, hair long, still very dark and, though getting thin, falls in such a way as to give a peculiar beauty to the mystic head'.[156] Blanche Warre-Cornish, who was related to Thackeray, also registered 'the consummate beauty of Tennyson's pose of head', regretted that 'strong glasses, necessary to his sight, sealed up the light that was so often in his eyes', and observed the 'hard lines . . . near the mouth, which, like his grave motion, marked him as a man of sorrows'.[157] (That last phrase had been used, long ago, by his brother Frederick with reference to their father.)

The coming of photography and of illustrated periodicals during Tennyson's lifetime meant that those who met him found themselves comparing the reality with the mental images they had already formed. R. C. Jebb, a Cambridge don and later a famous Greek scholar, judged him 'exactly like his photographs – I mean quite as shaggy. His long black hair is very thin now [1867]; he is bald on the crown; and it falls as from a tonsure about his ears. He looks older than I should have expected; his accent is decidedly Lincolnshire, and this was one of the things that surprised me'.[158] Jebb adds that 'It is impossible not to like him, and not to understand that he is a man of genius', and many accounts make the point that the impressiveness, even massiveness, of Tennyson's physical presence was matched by a sense of his being in other than physical respects profoundly different from other men. Suggesting that the portraits fail to convey 'the singular majesty of his figure', Edmund Gosse, who met him in 1871, felt a kind of apartness or remoteness about him: 'He stood there as we approached him, very still, with slightly dropping eyelids, and made no movement, no gesture of approach. When I had been presented, and had shaken his hand, he continued to consider me in a silence which would have been deeply disconcerting if it had not, somehow, seemed kindly, and even, absurd as it sounds, rather shy'.[159]

One facet of this remoteness was an almost wholly unconscious unconventionality, evident in his appearance and dress and in some of the possible apocryphal anecdotes of his *farouche* social behaviour. Another was a kind of innocence or unworldliness – at least this is how many saw it, though there were one or two dissidents. Jane Harrison resolutely declined to be taken in: 'He met us at the station, grunting fiercely that he "was not going to dress for dinner because I had come". It was rather frightening, but absurd. The vain old thing (he was the most openly vain man I ever met) knew quite well that he looked his best in his ample poet's cloak . . .'.[160] But the majority verdict is rather different. Sydney Dobell, 'Spasmodic' poet, wrote after a visit that he had 'found the glorious old god as godlike as ever . . . Nothing could be kinder than both Mr. and Mrs. Tennyson – he in his great blind superhuman manner, like a colossal child – and his often repeated disappointment that we could not stay longer near them was evidently as unfeigned and straight-spoken as everything, large and little, that comes out of that mouth, with which he rather seems to think aloud than, in the ordinary acceptation, to speak'. Jowett also speaks of him as a kind of superhuman child: after his 'annual visit' in 1861, he wrote that 'The more I see of him the more I respect his character, notwithstanding a superficial irritability and uneasiness about all things . . . No one is more honest, truthful, manly, or a warmer friend; but he is as open as the day, and, like a child, tells any chance comer what is passing in his mind'. Like Dobell's suggestion that he thought aloud rather than conversing, this seems to point to a surprising but fundamental social immaturity, an unawareness of how his behaviour might be seen or felt by others. Jowett adds perceptively: 'He is the shyest person I ever knew, feeling sympathy and needing it to a degree quite painful. Please not to repeat this to the vulgar, who can never be made to understand that great mental troubles necessarily accompany such powers as he possesses'.[161] Tennyson is indeed a particularly good illustration of the truth that the tenure of great powers exacts a price from the holder, or from others, or from both. What is much rarer is for genius to have the good fortune to find so many others prepared to make sacrifices in large or small ways, from the selfless devotion of Emily and Hallam to the visitors who found themselves required to conform to a household routine that had been devised to safeguard the poet's serenity of mind. Perhaps only in the Victorian age could such faith in the nobility of self-sacrifice or such deference to the imperative demands of genius have been possible.

The *Tiresias* volume of 1885 has been referred to in defiance of chronology, for it

74 The opening line of 'The Revenge' – published in Nineteenth Century *in March 1878 and included in the 1880 collection – in Tennyson's hand. According to the* Memoir, *this line 'was on my father's desk for years, but he finished the ballad at last all at once in a day or two'. (In his note here, Hallam Tennyson wrote in pencil: 'This line lay on A.T.s desk for years, before he began The Revenge' H.T.)*

was preceded by *Ballads and Other Poems* (1880). This was Tennyson's first volume of poetry for eight years (the dramas intervening), and it illustrates his tendency in his later years to limit himself to shorter poems. There is, however, a considerable variety of subject matter and forms: 'The Revenge' is a historical and patriotic ballad; 'Battle of Brunanburh' a translation from the Anglo-Saxon based partly on a prose translation published by Hallam Tennyson; 'The Defence of Lucknow' is based on an event in recent history (during the Indian Mutiny of 1857); 'The Northern Cobbler' and 'The Village Wife' are Lincolnshire dialect poems; 'In the Children's Hospital' is a dramatic monologue that combines social indignation with sentiment; 'The Voyage of Maeldune' is based on an Irish legend that Tennyson had come across in P. W. Joyce's *Old Celtic Romances* (1879); and 'Rizpah', originally titled 'Bones', which moved Swinburne to rhapsodical flights of eulogy, is a tale of maternal love based on an incident of the late eighteenth century. Despite its biblical title, the last of these is a tragedy of modern life (Tennyson had come across the anecdote in a magazine) – another dramatic monologue uttered this time by a simple but impassioned old woman not unlike Dickens's Betty Higden (another favourite of Swinburne's, who seems to have been partial to old women in dire straits):

They would scratch him up – they would hang him again on the cursed tree.
Sin? O yes – we are sinners, I know – let all that be,
And read me a Bible verse of the Lord's good will toward men –
'Full of compassion and mercy, the Lord' – let me hear it again;
'Full of compassion and mercy – long-suffering.' Yes, O yes!
For the lawyer is born but to murder – the Saviour lives but to bless.
*He*'ll never put on the black cap except for the worst of the worst,
And the first may be last – I have heard it in church – and the last may be first.
Suffering – O long-suffering – yes, as the Lord must know,
Year after year in the mist and the wind and the shower and the snow.

There is also, among so much fancy dress and so much inspired by literary sources, the touchingly personal 'To the Rev. W. H. Brookfield', commemorating the death in 1874 of his college friend. This sonnet, in which Arthur Hallam once more makes a brief appearance, has a noteworthy directness of feeling and language:

> You man of humorous-melancholy mark,
> Dead of some inward agony – is it so?
> Our kindlier, trustier Jaques, past away!
> I cannot laud this life, it looks so dark: . . .
> God bless you. I shall join you in a day.

Five years later, *Tiresias and Other Poems* notably includes not only 'To E. FitzGerald' but 'Despair', a dramatic monologue expressing, as Ricks says, the 'horror at a Godless universe and at a belief in eternal torment' which were 'lifelong preoccupations' of Tennyson's.[162] The title poem had been begun as early as 1833 and was taken up again and completed exactly fifty years later: as Emily told Edward Lear on 14 August 1883, 'Ally has been finishing one of his old world poems begun about the *Ulysses* period'[163] – though she might with greater appositeness have called it the Arthur Hallam period.

Between the publication of these two volumes, in 1883, Tennyson had at last

*75 Design for Tennyson's coat of arms. The motto means 'Looking backward, looking forward'.*

accepted an honour from the Queen. His full title became Baron Tennyson of Aldworth and Freshwater, and the barony had been bestowed, after prolonged negotiations, in December, announcements appearing in the press on the 10th of that month. Earlier offers had been declined, Tennyson making it clear that he wished for no honour for himself but would not mind securing a title for Hallam. Gladstone had formally advised the Queen on 20 September 'to permit the offer of a Barony to Mr Tennyson'; Victoria's reply three days later somewhat tartly reminded Gladstone that Disraeli had 'first proposed him for a Baronetcy wh[ich] he then did not wish for'.[164] Either her memory or her prejudice misled her, however, for Disraeli's approach in December 1874 had been preceded by a similar approach from Gladstone in March 1873.

76 Punch *cartoon, 22 December 1883. Tennyson's elevation to the peerage had been announced earlier in the month.*

The honour did not produce universal delight, and one or two accusing fingers were pointed at Emily. Knowles is said to have told a fellow guest at Wilton House that 'the literary world were very sorry about it and pitied the Poet Laureate for having fallen a victim to the ambition of his wife and eldest son', and Tennyson's brother Frederick wrote sardonically to his own son: 'Mrs. – now Baroness T. of Aldworth and Freshwater – has not been laid upon her back most of her life without nursing ambitious dreams, now realised'.[165] Martin cautiously concludes that 'it is hard to deny a grain of truth in his overstatement of the case'.[166] As it turned out, Tennyson himself was not wholly indifferent to his new honour, and announced himself on the title page of the 1885 volume as 'Alfred Lord Tennyson'. He took his seat in the House of Lords in March 1884, 'on the cross benches', as Hallam wrote in his journal, 'for he could not pledge himself to party'.[167]

1883 had in any case been a year in which Tennyson had moved in the highest circles. The Queen consulted him about an inscription for the memorial to her 'faithful attendant and friend' John Brown; of his four suggestions she rejected those by Shakespeare, Pope and Byron in favour of an anonymous three-line encomium which she quite correctly surmised to be from her Laureate's own pen. In August he visited Osborne and spent nearly an hour with the Queen in Albert's room; she noted afterwards that he was 'very shaky on his legs' but she had perhaps made excessive demands on the ability of a man who had just had his 74th birthday to remain standing for a long period. Her journal notes that she 'told him what a comfort "In Memoriam" had again been to me which pleased him'.[168]

In September Tennyson and Hallam joined a party on the *Pembroke Castle*, a new ship belonging to the politician and shipping magnate Sir Donald Currie. Among their fellow passengers were the Gladstones. From Barrow they sailed round the northern coast of Scotland and across to Norway and Denmark. The Prince of Wales, the Czar and Czarina of Russia, the King and Queen of Greece, and numerous other royal and noble persons were staying with the King of Denmark at this time, and on 18 September the whole party came to lunch on board. Tennyson sat next to the Queen of Greece, and the Queen of Denmark proposed a toast to him. Afterwards he gave a short reading, and this was the occasion on which his myopia led him to commit a celebrated *faux pas*: as he later told a friend, 'When I finished reading, [a] lady [sitting beside me on the sofa] said something very civil, and I thought she was Andrew Clark's daughter, so I patted her on the shoulder very affectionately, and said, "My dear girl, that's very kind of you, very kind." I heard the Czar chuckling mightily to himself, so I looked more nearly at her, and, God bless me! 't was the Czarina herself'.[169]

At an earlier stage of the cruise, Tennyson had read regularly 'in the mornings and evenings' to the party on board, and had been 'very much offended' by Gladstone's falling asleep during one such reading.[170] More acceptably, Gladstone and Tennyson had shared memories of Arthur Hallam, whose ghost, half a century after his death, seems never to have been very far away.

Two more volumes of verse followed in 1886 and 1889. The title poem of the first, *Locksley Hall Sixty Years After*, is another example of Tennyson's habit in his later work of drawing on his early emotional capital: the experiences of youth, its friendships and its poems. The original 'Locksley Hall', a poem of the late 1830s, had at first included the following lines, dropped from the final version:

> In the hall there hangs a painting – Amy's arms about my neck –
> Happy children in a sunbeam sitting on the ribs of wreck.
>
> In my life there was a picture, she that clasped my neck had flown;
> I was left within the shadow sitting on the wreck alone.

These, according to Tennyson, became the nucleus of the later poem. The speaker of this dramatic monologue, 'this old white-headed dreamer', not only recalls the past and laments the deaths of loved ones but attacks contemporary social evils, including, in one shrill passage (lines 137–45), the new literary realism:

> Feed the budding rose of boyhood with the drainage of your sewer;
> Send the drain into the fountain, lest the stream should issue pure.
>
> Set the maiden fancies wallowing in the troughs of Zolaism . . .

There was certainly a case by the 1880s for questioning the myth of progress, and others had already done so, but this is too much like Dickens's Mr Podsnap to be effective. Among the old man's other subjects are developments in science, including astronomy('. . . and the sun himself will pass') and evolutionary theory; urban growth ('Science grows and Beauty dwindles – roofs of slated hideousness!'); child neglect, prostitution, sweated labour, the disposal of the dead, infectious diseases, and poor housing ('And the crowded couch of incest in the warrens of the poor') – all these last half-dozen topics in seven lines! It is, perhaps, *un peu trop*, and W. W. Robson has gone so far as to condemn the poem as 'disastrously bad'.

Although it is, strictly speaking, a dramatic monologue and can claim to be read as an objective portrayal of a fictional character, it is impossible to accept Tennyson's statement that '*There is not one touch of biography* [i.e. autobiography] *in it from beginning to end*',[170] and impossible not to believe that he is giving vent in it to his sense of the age he had lived to see as deeply uncongenial. The great Victorian had become a late Victorian whether he liked it or not (and on the whole he did not): by 1886 Hardy, Gissing, Kipling and others of a new and very different generation were launched on their careers, and for some the Age of Tennyson was already giving way to the Age of Wilde. If we are looking for evidence that Tennyson's finest poems in his later years are personal and intimate rather than public and rhetorical, 'Locksley Hall Sixty Years After' strengthens the case.

In other ways Tennyson's protestation (suspicious by virtue of its very vehemence) that the poem is purely an 'imaginative edifice' cannot be taken seriously. 'Gone the tyrant of my youth' refers to his grandfather (and the following line [44] glances sardonically at the eulogistic memorial erected by Tennyson's uncle); the poem's Edith is the dedicatee of the volume, Emily; 'our sailor son . . . Leonard early lost at sea' is unmistakably the recently dead (for poetic control *too* recently dead) Lionel. Once again, though, what is striking is the interweaving of the powerful emotional experiences of a whole lifetime.

*Demeter and Other Poems* (1889) includes as its final item the later and fuller poetic memorial to Lionel already referred to, as well as three of the quiet-voiced, delicately poised poems to loved individuals that are characteristic of the best of Tennyson's final period. 'To Ulysses' is addressed to W. G. Palgrave, brother of the anthologist. 'To Mary Boyle', a verse-epistle somewhat in the manner of Horace and Jonson,

*77 Cartoon in the* Illustrated London News, *12 December 1889. The caption reads: 'THE TWO POETS. By a strange coincidence new volumes of poetry by our two great living poets will be published almost on the same day.' The volumes were Browning's* Asolando *and Tennyson's* Demeter and Other Poems. *By an even stranger coincidence, Browning died in Italy on the day the cartoon appeared. Tennyson's volume sold 20,000 copies in the first week. He was one of those who urged the Dean of Westminster Abbey that Browning should be buried in Poet's Corner, and Hallam acted for him as one of the pall-bearers at the funeral.*

again links past and present and imposes a pattern on the flow of time by introducing a poem Tennyson had written 'more than half a hundred years ago' ('The Progress of Poesy') but never published. Here, as repeatedly, one has an impressive sense of the whole of Tennyson's richly productive creative lifetime forming a single fabric, so that he can refer to a poem of fifty years earlier as he might refer to an earlier passage in the same poem. 'To Mary Boyle' also demonstrated that he had lost none of his old

*78 Photograph by Barraud (c. 1888), taken for the series 'Men and Women of the Day'.*

magic for catching in a brief phrase some exact and beautiful observation of the natural world, as in

> Our elmtree's ruddy-hearted blossom-flake
>> Is fluttering down

and

> And all the gold from each laburnum chain
>> Drop to the grass

and

> A rhyme that flowered betwixt the whitening sloe
>> And kingcup blaze . . .

The shortest of these three poems, and perhaps the finest, is 'The Roses on the Terrace': the 'Rose' is Rosa Baring of Harrington Hall, another memory from half a century past, her name melting into the 'red rose' that blossoms before his aged eyes as well as, in memory, into the blush remembered from their youth, just as the Aldworth terrace dissolves into the terrace of the Lincolnshire mansion:

> Rose, on this terrace fifty years ago,
>> When I was in my June, you in your May,
> Two words, '*My* Rose', set all your face aglow,
>> And now that I am white, and you are gray,
> That blush of fifty years ago, my dear,
>> Blooms in the Past, but close to me today
> As this red rose, which on our terrace here
>> Glows in the blue of fifty miles away.

As in 'To E. FitzGerald', the workings of memory, bringing together what is widely separated in place and time, are conveyed through superb syntactical control in this one-sentence poem, just as the final phrase looks into a distance that is not merely spatial. Ricks nominates 'To E. FitzGerald' as his favourite Tennyson poem, 'if one may distinguish the favourite from the best';[171] my own vote would be for 'The Roses on the Terrace' as the most perfect and, within its eight lines, the most subtle among them all.

In the same collection, old magic is again in question in 'Merlin and the Gleam', a reminder that Tennyson's infatuation with the Arthurian stories had itself extended over more than half a century. There is a process at work by which Tennyson had come to identify himself with the Arthurian magician (Ricks notes that he had signed a poem 'Merlin' as early as 1852[172]), and the myth-making must have been at least partly conscious. 'Merlin and the Gleam' is clearly retrospective and valedictory, one of those works in which a writer looks back over a lifetime that he knows cannot be much longer extended, though the autobiographical allegory remains somewhat obscure:

> Once at the croak of a Raven who crost it,
> A barbarous people,
> Blind to the magic,
> And deaf to the melody,
> Snarled at and cursed me.
> A demon vext me,
> The light retreated,
> The landskip darkened,
> The melody deadened,
> The Master whispered
> 'Follow the gleam.'

The references here have been variously interpreted as pointing to the hostile critics of the 1832 volume and to the family distresses in the period following his father's

GORDON

FOR THE
GORDON BOYS'
HOME

79 Punch *cartoon, 15 August 1891. Tennyson is not named but is presumed to be instantly recognisable. Shortly after General Gordon's death at Khartoum in January 1885, Tennyson had joined the committee set up to establish a Gordon Cadet Corps. A Gordon Boys' Home had been founded, and in August 1891 Tennyson had written to the* Daily Telegraph *urging readers to subscribe to the fund. Later, boys from the Home were among those present at Tennyson's funeral.*

death. (It is tempting, though not irresistibly so, to read 'croak' as an allusion to J. W. Croker, the *Quarterly*'s severe reviewer.) Whichever interpretation is preferred, the striking thing is that after nearly half a century these grievances were still fresh in Tennyson's mind.

There was to be one more volume of poems, the just-posthumous *The Death of Oenone, Akbar's Dream, and Other Poems*, and it might as well be dealt with here. This slim volume appeared on 28 October 1892, some three weeks after Tennyson's death, and contains some very late examples of his work. 'The Death of Oenone', written in 1889–90, is a sequel to 'Oenone'. 'June Bracken and Heather', which stands first, serves as a dedication to Emily (though she is not actually named) and was written in June 1891. It seems a pity that the last piece in his last volume should be a specimen of laureate fustian, 'The Death of the Duke of Clarence and Avondale': Victoria's grandson had died in January 1892 at the age of 28, and though he is no longer thought to have been Jack the Ripper his character and reputation make Tennyson's encomium ('So princely, tender, truthful, reverent, pure . . .') ring decidedly hollow. So much, at least, with the benefit of hindsight, but before we hasten to convict Tennyson of hypocrisy or sycophancy we should remind ourselves, as the editors of the *Letters* point out, that 'The real questions are: "What did Tennyson know, and when did he know it?"'[173] The poem had appeared, in prompt response to the Duke's death, in the *Nineteenth Century* in February 1892.

By this time Tennyson's own death was not far distant. He had had a serious illness – his first – during the winter of 1888–9; Hallam describes it as 'a bad attack of rheumatic gout . . . brought on chiefly by walking in the rain and storm, and getting drenched', and adds that it was followed by 'two bad relapses'.[174] It seems to have extended from September to May and in a man of nearly eighty must have given great cause for concern. Hallam's list of the books his father asked to have read to him during his illness gives some idea of the range of his interests: 'Leaf's edition of the *Iliad*; the *Iphigenia in Aulis*, expressing "wonder at its modernness"; Matthew Arnold on Tolstoi; Fiske's *Destiny of Man*; Gibbon's History, especially praising the

*Fall of Constantinople*; Keats' poems; Wordsworth's "Recluse"'. Hallam does not mention any novels, but we can assume that they were also on the menu, for Tennyson was a great novel-reader – a passionate admirer of Jane Austen, for instance (he compared her to Shakespeare), as well as of Scott and Thackeray, but also with a keen appetite for the more sensational varieties of contemporary fiction: he once described himself as 'simply steeped in Miss Braddon', the author of the best-seller *Lady Audley's Secret*.

A glimpse of Tennyson during his illness comes from the always vivid and engaging diary of his old friend Allingham, who visited Aldworth on 3 November 1888:

> Up to study, and found T. leaning back on a chair, his legs on another, thin and pale; he gave me his brown hand and said 'I'm glad to see you.'
>
> He had a book in his hand, and the light of two candles close by fell on the right side of his face, which showed striking and noble. He wore a black skull-cap, his long Don Quixote nose was sharply outlined, his moustache looked dark and full. By general impression one might have guessed him seventy rather than eighty.[175]

They discussed, among other things, Zola ('[Tennyson's] question "How can a book corrupt?"') and Martial ('"Are these books necessary for the learning of Latin?"'). Allingham himself died in November 1889, soon after Tennyson's 80th birthday, a landmark which elicited congratulations from the Queen and countless others.

Another visitor, present at one of his last readings in June 1892, has given a portrait of Tennyson in the final months of his life:

> No picture I have ever seen of him has, to my mind, conveyed his face. The delicately refined features are known to us all, but the look of youth that came into his eyes as he read, and the loveableness of his personality, had been

*80 Portrait of Tennyson (1890) by Helen Allingham, wife of his friend William Allingham, who had died in the previous year.*

conveyed to me by no picture. I could only say to myself 'Yes, this is Tennyson, and just what I should have wished him to be.' He was so entirely the reverse of formidable that day, so winning, simple, and sincere . . .

His reading cannot be described. It was an interpretation and revelation. His voice melodious and full of change, and quite unimpaired by age. There was a peculiar freshness and passion in his reading, giving the impression that he had just written the poem and that the emotion which created it was fresh in him . . .[176]

His last reading of *Maud* was given on 24 August, six weeks before his death.

In the early summer he had been fit enough to go with Hallam on a short cruise to the Channel Islands and they visited Tennyson's brother Frederick, who was living in Jersey. At the end of June he left Farringford for the last time, and some of the events of the next few weeks have a flavour of valediction. In September, for instance, Hallam was sent to Somersby, where the old Tennyson home was for sale, to bring back a report on it to his father. Visitors had been numerous in the previous month, when Tennyson had celebrated his 83rd birthday, but in September Emily tried to discourage them as her husband grew weaker. He took his last drive on 28 September; perhaps it was too much for him, for his condition thereafter deteriorated and he sank steadily, dying at 1.35 a.m. on Thursday, 6 October.

And so this narrative reaches the point at which it started, the picturesque deathbed that was so singularly appropriate for the man Tennyson had become during the second half of his lifetime. His death, and his funeral six days later in Westminster Abbey, received (to use a most un-Victorian phrase) the full media coverage that might have been anticipated. The *Illustrated London News*, for instance, published on 15 October a long and lavishly illustrated section devoted to the poet's life, works, homes and haunts. On 7 October *The Times* printed, with rather suspicious promptness, a substantial – or at any rate long-winded – poem, 'The Passing of Merlin', by Alfred Austin, the poetaster who was to succeed Tennyson in the

81 'Crossing the Bar', published in Punch on 15 October 1892, three days after Tennyson's funeral, and referring to the poem of which Tennyson himself declared, 'Mind you put my Crossing the Bar at the end of all editions of my poems'.

176

Laureateship. (It was in effect a political appointment, and the fact that over three years elapsed before it was made strongly suggests that Tennyson was felt to be irreplaceable.) Austin's title, like Robert Buchanan's reference to Tennyson in another poem as 'the Galahad of Song', points to a significant confusion of the poet and his characters. Auden was to say on Yeats's death that he had become his admirers but Tennyson, it seems, had become his poems. Artists as well as versifiers were kept busy during these October weeks, and the press carried numerous depictions of the deathbed, the Abbey ceremony, and much else.

In the throng outside the Abbey, street-vendors were offering pictures of Tennyson and copies of 'Crossing the Bar', priced sixpence: this was the poem that Tennyson had composed in October 1889 while crossing from the mainland to the Isle of Wight ('in twenty minutes', according to his later account) and had instructed should be placed 'at the end of all editions of my poems'.[177] Inside the pall-bearers included two prime ministers, an ambassador, a duke and the Master of Trinity; poets were in relatively short supply, but the well-known novelist Thomas Hardy was present and afterwards noted in his diary the impression that it was all a bit overdone and 'less penetrating than a plain country interment would have been'.[178] Emily, unable to stand the strain, was not present. But during what remained of her life (a little less than four years) she worked hard to assist Hallam with the preparation of the *Memoir*, a suitably massive memorial to Tennyson's huge achievement.

As if mocking the labours of biographers, Tennyson's grave in Poet's Corner bears (apart from his name) only the dates of his birth and death. Browning lies on one side of him, T. S. Eliot on the other; nearby lie his friends Edward Lear, Lewis Carroll and George Eliot as well as G. M. Hopkins, who thought much of his poetry Parnassian, Henry James, who found him 'not Tennysonian', and W. H. Auden, who declared him the stupidest of all English poets. In the phrase Auden used of Yeats, his gift has outlived all these opinions.

# EPILOGUE

‘TENNYSON'S BIOGRAPHY,’ OBSERVED LASCELLES Abercrombie in 1931, ‘is, on the whole, uninteresting.’[179] Even granted that less was known sixty years ago about the bizarre drama of Tennyson's family background and early years, this seems an infelicitous judgement. It is surely, even in its broad outlines, a life of a striking shape and pattern, embodying both startling contrasts and a remarkable consistency. From obscurity to the highest fame; from depression and hypochondria and thoughts of suicide to stability, self-confidence and a kind of serenity; from the crowded rectory in darkest Lincolnshire to Osborne, Windsor Castle, and the company of the crowned heads of Europe on the *Pembroke Castle*: it is both a Victorian success story and the personal background to what Eric Griffiths has called ‘an astonishing persistence of creative endeavour’.[180] Few, whether poets or not, settle so early on a vocation and pursue it so unwaveringly for so long. It is, moreover, a life with an uncanny symmetry: marriage at its midpoint transformed his outer and inner existence by freeing him from (in a phrase used by the editor of Emily's letters) ‘the prison of selfhood’.[181] In many respects it is a life that seems constructed like a work of art. If in its later stages it turned Tennyson into an almost legendary figure, that of Poet or Bard, he himself may not have been altogether unaware or unwilling to respond to his age's demand for heroes.

Nowadays, while not demanding heroes, we often expect our great writers to be

*82 Statue of Tennyson by G. F. Watts.*
*It stands outside Lincoln Cathedral and was unveiled on 15 July 1905;*
*Watts had died in the previous year.*

decent and likeable men and women, and are disappointed or indignant when they quarrel with their spouses, treat their friends badly, are mean with money, or otherwise fall short of our high expectations. Not many unwritten lives, perhaps, could live up to such demands, but while Tennyson has sometimes been charged with egotism, vanity and meanness, his character stands up reasonably well to the prolonged scrutiny to which modern no-holds-barred biographical enquiry has subjected him. If he could on occasion behave a little reprehensibly in (for instance) continuing to draw his Civil List pension long after he achieved wealth, he could also be generous beyond the call of duty: in 1871 he sent the substantial sum of £200 to an impecunious poet, Robert Buchanan, who had asked for his assistance. By a large number of his friends he was not only admired but loved, and not only loved but revered. There is little need to invoke the argument that genius cannot be expected to conform to the normal standards of decent behaviour: Tennyson's genius is not in doubt, but his fundamental integrity and uprightness and his deep capacity for friendship are constantly in evidence.

He enjoyed the fruits of fame but never courted celebrity – on the contrary, he loathed many of its results and sought in vain to remain a private man when the world wished to beat a path to his door. His popularity was of a kind difficult to grasp in an age when poetry has lost its central place in the cultural life of the nation; judging by sales of his published works it may have waned in his later years, but generalisations about popularity can always be misleading since at any given moment one generation's idol can be another's has-been. There are innumerable Tennyson Roads and Tennyson Avenues in the small towns of England, and he is still one of a small handful of poets of whom virtually everyone has heard even if they cannot quote a single line. He wins 339 entries in the *Oxford Dictionary of Quotations*.

For much of the nineteenth century and for at least a generation after his death he was by any mode of reckoning *the* modern English poet. The reaction in the earlier part of this century was almost inevitable and was suffered by other Victorian giants such as Dickens and George Eliot. The modernist poets made fashionable a kind of poetry that was not Tennyson's kind – was indeed almost its opposite in every respect – and new critical methods were ill suited to dealing with the longer poetic forms in which so much of his work was cast. While the Metaphysicals and the Modernists gained from this, Tennyson, and the Victorians in general, lost. Since then, a more tolerant, eclectic, accommodating criticism has rediscovered Tennyson and he has been permitted by general consent to reoccupy his place as the greatest of Victorian poets. This has not been, however, simply a return to the status quo, for the Tennyson we most value is in many respects different from the one most loudly applauded by his contemporaries. Few now read and mark *In Memoriam* as a personal guide to conduct and belief; 'Enoch Arden' no longer reduces us to hysterics; schoolgirls no longer copy portions of the *Idylls of the King* into their commonplace books, nor do artists depict Tennysonian scenes on large canvases. Tennyson the moralist and teacher is admired less highly than the introspective, self-absorbed poet who can project his emotions upon a landscape and evoke that landscape with delicate particularity and poignant effectiveness. Certain moods, scenes, seasons and kinds of weather have been appropriated for the unmistakable Tennysonian note, to which certain kinds of verbal music, verse-movement and cadence also contribute. His range may not be wide but within its limits his effects are powerful and memorable. One would add that it is inimitable if it had not so often been imitated, not least by parodists whose attentions constitute a kind of oblique recognition of a highly personal manner as well as a widespread familiarity. Browning could complain of the psychological shallowness of one of the Arthurian poems, 'Pelleas and Ettarre': 'I should judge the conflict in the knight's soul the proper subject to describe; Tennyson thinks he should describe the castle, and the effect of the moon on its towers, and anything *but* the soul'. But he was also impelled on another occasion to say of Tennyson what stands as an epigraph to this brief life: 'Nobody has more fully found out at the beginning what he was born to do – nor done it more perfectly'.[182] It is handsomely said and can hardly be gainsaid.

# NOTES

THE FOLLOWING ABBREVIATIONS HAVE BEEN USED IN THE NOTES:

*Memoir*      [Hallam Tennyson], *Alfred Lord Tennyson: A Memoir by his Son* (London: Macmillan, 1897), 2 vols.

*Letters*      *The Letters of Alfred Lord Tennyson*, ed. Cecil Y. Lang & Edgar F. Shannon Jr (Oxford: Clarendon Press, 1982–90), 3 vols.

*EF Letters*      *The Letters of Edward FitzGerald*, ed. Alfred McKinley Terhune & Annabelle Burdick Terhune (Princeton, N.J.: Princeton University Press, 1980), 4 vols.

CT      Charles Tennyson, *Alfred Tennyson* (London: Macmillan, 1949).

Jump      *Tennyson: The Critical Heritage*, ed. John D. Jump (London: Routledge & Kegan Paul, 1967).

Martin      Robert Bernard Martin, *Tennyson: The Unquiet Heart* (Oxford: Clarendon Press, 1980).

Ricks      Christopher Ricks, *Tennyson* (London: Macmillan, 1972).

*Poems*      *The Poems of Tennyson . . . Incorporating the Trinity College Manuscripts*, ed. Christopher Ricks (London: Longman, 1987), 3 vols. (Second edition, revised and expanded, of the work published in 1969.)

1. *Memoir*, II, 428–9.

2. Letters, III, 11. Compare Thomas Woolner's remark in a letter dated 5 December 1859: 'I grieve to hear that the Poet is not well . . .'.

3. Muriel Spark & Derek Stanford, *Emily Brontë: Her Life and Work* (London: Peter Owen, 1953), 11–12.

4. The letter is dated 18 March 1833 (*Letters*, I, 90).

5. *Tennyson at Aldworth: The Diary of James Henry Mangles*, ed. Earl A. Knies (Athens, Ohio: Ohio University Press, 1984), 50.

6. Martin, 10.

7. Ann C. Colley, *Tennyson and Madness* (Athens, Ga.: University of Georgia Press, 1983), 34.

8. *Letters*, I, 106.

9. W. H. Auden, *Tennyson: An Introduction and a Selection* (London: Phoenix House, 1946), x.

10. Charles Tennyson & Hope Dyson, *The Tennysons: Background to Genius* (London: Macmillan, 1974), 195.

11. Martin, 26.

12. Martin, 7.

13. Charles Tennyson, *Alfred Tennyson and Somersby* (Lincoln: Tennyson Society, 1974) (not paginated).

14. *Memoir*, I, 11, 4.

15. *Memoir*, I, 6.

16. *Memoir*, I, 11–12. Some of the same information is given, with slight variations of detail, in a letter of Tennyson's dated 2 December 1872 (Letters, III, 44–5).

17. *Letters*, I, 14.

18. *Memoir*, I, 35.

19. Martin, 69, 73.

20. *Letters*, I, 14, 29, 31.

21. Quoted in *Poems*, I, 189–90

22. CT, 82–3.

23. Peter Allen, *The Cambridge Apostles: The Early Years* (Cambridge: Cambridge University Press, 1978), 130.

24. *Ibid.*, 133.

25. Jump, 87.

26. Ricks, 40.

27. Quoted in Ricks, 65.

28. Martin, 120.

29. Sir Charles Tennyson, *Six Tennyson Essays* (London: Macmillan, 1954), 39–40, 55.

30. *Letters*, I, 59.

31. *Memoir*, I, 196.

32. *Letters*, II, 290.

33. *Memoir*, I, 107.

34. Cecil Y. Lang, *Tennyson's Arthurian Psychodrama* (Lincoln: Tennyson Society), 1983, 1.

35. *Poems*, II, 305; Lang, *op. cit.*, 3. On the circumstances of Hallam's death, see Jack Kolb, 'Morte d'Arthur: the Death of Arthur Hallam', *Biography*, 9 (1986), 37–58.

36. Marion Shaw, *An Annotated Critical Bibliography of Alfred, Lord Tennyson* (Hemel Hempstead: Harvester Wheatsheaf, 1989), 13.

37. *Letters*, I, 87.

38. Brian Southam, *Tennyson* (London: Longman, 1971), 24.

39. Quoted in *Poems*, II, 307.

40. Jump, 2.

41. Quoted in Martin, 172.

42. Jump, 3.

43. *Ibid.*

44. Ricks, 147.

45. Quoted in Martin, 189.

46. Robert Bernard Martin, *With Friends Possessed: A Life of Edward FitzGerald* (London: Faber & Faber, 1985), 181.

47. *EF Letters*, I, 162.

48. *Ibid.*, 166.

49. Quoted in Martin, 210.

50. Martin, 211.

51. Quoted in Martin, 415.

52. *Letters*, I, 130.

53. *Memoir*, I, 166.

54. Martin, 266–7.

55. *Letters*, I, 157.

56. Quoted in F. B. Pinion, *A Tennyson Chronology* (London: Macmillan, 1990), 28; *Tennyson: Interviews and Recollections*, ed. Norman Page (London: Macmillan, 1983), 6, 8, 12; Martin, 242.

57. *EF Letters*, I, 290.

58. *Letters*, I, 203.

59. *EF Letters*, I, 272.

60. *Ibid.*, 315.

61. *Ibid.*, 272, 494; CT, 191.

62. Ricks, 177; Martin, 265.

63. Martin, 290 (Wordsworth had talent-spotted Tennyson on a visit to Trinity as early as 1830, when he had noted that 'Two brothers of the name of Tennyson, in particular, are not a little promising': Martin, 126); *The Collected Letters of Thomas and Jane Welsh Carlyle*, Vol. XV, ed. C. de L. Ryals & K. J. Fielding (Durham N.C.: Duke University Press, 1987), 216; *The Letters of Charles Dickens*, Vol. III, ed. Madeline House, Graham Storey, & Kathleen Tillotson (Oxford: Clarendon Press, 1974), 306, 460 (letters of 7 August 1842, 9 March 1843).

64. Jump, 5–6.

65. *Letters*, I, 204.

66. *Ibid.*, 68, 159.

67. *EF Letters*, I, 246.

68. *The Correspondence of Emerson and Carlyle*, ed. Joseph Slater (New York: Columbia University Press, 1964), 363.

69. *Letters*, I, 222–3.

70. *Ibid.*, 232.

71. *Ibid.*, 238.

72. *EF Letters*, I, 559.

73. Quoted in *Poems*, II, 186.

74. *William Allingham's Diary* (Fontwell: Centaur Press, 1967), 301.

75. *Letters*, I, 239.

76. *Ibid.*, 283.

77. *EF Letters*, I, 623.

78. *Memoir*, I, 243.

79. *The Letters of Emily Lady Tennyson*, ed. James O. Hoge (University Park: Pennsylvania State University Press, 1974), 44.

80. *Letters*, II, 331.

81. *Memoir*, I, 329.

82. *Letters*, I, 335.

83. *Ibid.*, 339–40.

84. Jump, 8.

85. *Punch*, XVIII (1850), 241.

86. *Letters*, I, 342, n2.

87. *EF Letters*, II, 408.

88. *Letters*, II, 5.

89. *Ibid.*, 14–15.

90. *Ibid.*, 86.

91. *Ibid.*, 37, 40.

92. *EF Letters*, II, 83.

93. *Letters*, II, 75.

94. Martin, 377.

95. *The Letters of Charles Dickens*, Vol. VI, ed. G. Storey, K. Tillotson & N. Burgis (Oxford: Clarendon Press, 1988), 764.

96. *Letters*, II, 114.

97. Jump, 248; see also *Memoir*, I, 398–9.

98. CT, 286.

99. R. W. Rader, *Tennyson's 'Maud': The Biographical Genesis* (Berkeley: University of California Press, 1963), 100.

100. Quoted in *Poems*, II, 517.

101. Quoted in Ricks, 261; Jump, 186.

102. Ricks, 246.

103. For another delightful account of a reading of *Maud*, see *William Allingham's Diary*, 117–18. See also Gordon N. Ray, *Tennyson Reads 'Maud'* (Vancouver: University of British Columbia Press, 1968), which has furnished a number of these quotations, and Eric Griffiths, *The Printed Voice of Victorian Poetry* (Oxford: Clarendon Press, 1989), especially Chapter 2.

104. Martin, 376.

105. *EF Letters*, II, 272.

106. *Letters*, II, 87.

107. N. Pevsner & D. Lloyd, *Hampshire and the Isle of Wight* (Harmondsworth: Penguin Books, 1967), 50.

108. Paul Hyland, *Wight: Biography of an Island* (London: Gollancz, 1984), 198.

109. *Letters*, II, 300, 383.

110. *Ibid.*, 456.

111. *Letters*, III, 11.

112. *Letters*, II, 531.

113. *Ibid.*, 530.

114. *Tennyson at Aldworth: The Diary of James Henry Mangles*, p. 29.

115. *Letters*, II, 177.

116. *Ibid.*

117. *Letters*, II, 204.

118. *Ibid.*, 205.

119. *Ibid.*, 391; *William Allingham's Diary*, 145.

120. *Letters*, III, 54.

121. *Letters*, II, 327.

122. *Ibid.*, 195.

123. Jump, 13.

124. CT, 351; P. G. Scott, *Tennyson's Enoch Arden: A Victorian Best-Seller* (Lincoln: Tennyson Society, 1970), 2.

125. Jump, 12.

126. *Ibid.*, 11; Martin, 424, 467.

127. CT, 425.

128. Letter of 12 May 1861 (Tennyson Research Centre).

129. *Lady Tennyson's Journal*, ed. James O. Hoge (Charlottesville: University of Virginia Press, 1981), 11.

130. *Letters*, III, 87.

131. *Ibid.*, 106, 107.

132. Thomas Hardy, *The Life and Work of Thomas Hardy*, ed. Michael Millgate (London: Macmillan, 1984), 140.

133. *William Allingham's Diary*, 340.

134. *Memoir*, II, 208.

135. *Letters*, III, 331.

136. *Ibid.*, 135–6.

137. *Memoir*, II, 167.

138. Elaine Jordan, *Alfred Tennyson* (Cambridge: Cambridge University Press, 1988), 21–2.

139. W. H. Auden, *Tennyson: An Introduction and a Selection*, x.

140. *Tennyson at Aldworth: The Diary of James Henry Mangles*, 85 (the diary entry is dated August 1871).

141. *Memoir*, II, 21–2; I, 374.

142. *Letters*, III, 136.

143. *William Allingham's Diary*, 215.

144. CT, 468.

145. *Ibid.*, 368.

146. *Memoir*, II, 90.

147. CT, 460.

148. Martin, 483.

149. CT, 460.

150. *Letters*, III, 152.

151. Robert Bernard Martin, *With Friends Possessed*, 279.

152. *EF Letters*, III, 705.

153. *The Poems of Tennyson*, ed. C. Ricks (London: Longmans, 1969), 1317.

154. Ricks, 293.

155. *Letters*, III, 398–9.

156. *Ibid.*, 267, 349, 439.

157. 'Memories of Tennyson', *London Mercury*, 5 (1921–2), 147.

158. *Letters*, III, 481.

159. *Tennyson: Interviews and Recollections*, ed. Norman Page, 125.

160. Jane Ellen Harrison, *Reminiscences of a Student's Life* (London: Hogarth Press, 1925), 46.

161. *Letters*, III, 270–1.

162. *Poems*, III, 87.

163. *Ibid.*, 568.

164. *Letters*, III, 260, 262.

165. *Ibid.*, 273.

166. Martin, 545.

# INDEX